INDIAN EPIGRAPHY

INDIAN EPIGRAPHY

THE INSCRIPTIONAL BASES OF INDIAN HISTORICAL RESEARCH

JOHN C. LOWRIE

GYAN

Published by

GYAN

Gyan Publishing House
5, Ansari Road
Daryaganj, New Delhi-110002
Phone: 011-47034999, 9811692060
E-mail: books@gyanbooks.com

Distribution Network
gyanbooks.com
India, USA, Canada, UK, Australia

ISBN: 978-93-7097-022-9 (PB)

First Published, 1907

2nd Impression 2025

Printed at: Gyan Press, Delhi.

INDIAN EPIGRAPHY
Arthur JOHN FAITHFULL FLEET

INDIAN EPIGRAPHY

THE INSCRIPTIONAL BASES OF INDIAN HISTORICAL RESEARCH

BY

JOHN FAITHFULL FLEET, C.I.E., Ph.D.

INDIAN CIVIL SERVICE (RETIRED)
MEMBER OF THE ROYAL ASIATIC SOCIETY
CORRESPONDING MEMBER OF THE ROYAL SOCIETY OF SCIENCES, GÖTTINGEN
HONORARY MEMBER OF THE GERMAN ORIENTAL SOCIETY

1907

CONTENTS

TABLE OF CONTENTS

THE INDIAN EMPIRE

HISTORICAL

CHAPTER I

EPIGRAPHY

I. Introductory Note

THE subject of this contribution to the Imperial Gazetteer is the explanation of the nature and value of the epigraphic or inscriptional bases of Indian research for the pre-Musalmān period. And the topic is an important one; for, not only is India particularly rich in inscriptional remains, but also those remains are the only sure grounds of historical results in every line of research connected with its ancient past. We have, however, to exclude from our treatment of this subject one branch which has always been found more generally attractive than any of the others. The inscriptions on coins and gems, better termed, by way of avoiding confusion, 'legends' on coins and gems, are epigraphic materials. But they are a special class of such materials; and the treatment of them falls, most properly, under the subdivision of numismatology. We have to confine our attention here to those epigraphic remains which have come to be best known as 'inscriptions' by way of distinction from the numismatic materials. Nevertheless, we hope to be able to show that our topic is no dry and dull one, but is full of interest as well as importance. Introductory note.

The inscriptions, thus indicated as our topic, are notifications, very frequently of an official character, and generally more or less of a public nature, which recite facts, simple or complex, with or without dates, and were intended to be lasting records of the matters to which they refer. They are in almost all cases found engraved, not written. They were occasionally engraved upon monuments in the shape of great monolithic columns; as, for instance, in the case of some of the moral and religious edicts of Aśōka, and the panegyric on the two columns of victory at Mandasōr, in Mālwā, which recites the conquests of king Yaśōdharman. Mostly, however, they are found engraved on metal plates, on stone tablets, on rocks, on walls and pillars and other parts of caves or of temples and other buildings, on pedestals of images and statues, and on relic-caskets. But they are occasionally found painted, and in a few instances written with ink. And some are found stamped on clay and bricks.

For the purposes that we have in view, the inscriptions include, with the exception of the legends on coins and gems, everything inscriptive, written, painted, stamped or engraved, public or private, lengthy or brief, that can be turned to account in connexion with the ancient past of India, in respect of the political history, the religious development, or any other line of research. Even the mere records of pilgrims' visits are of value, in establishing the antiquity of the sacred places visited by them, and of the towns from which they came. Even descriptive labels, incised as accompaniments to statues and sculptures, are valuable, in marking the ancient times to which traditions and legends and mythological notions may be carried back. Even a name stamped on a brick has been found of use, in determining the period to which a building may be referred. And even masons' marks, in the form of alphabetical characters, have played an important part in the inquiry into the history of writing in India.

Such are the remains with which we are to deal, and of which we shall speak either as 'inscriptions,' or as 'epigraphic records,' or simply as 'records,' according to the convenience of the moment. But we are to handle them to only a certain extent.

There are technical details connected with the inscriptions into the treatment of which we cannot, for various reasons, enter here. For the palaeographic branch of Indian epigraphic research, which explains the alphabets in which the inscriptions were written, and deals with the origin and development of those alphabets, we can here only refer to Professor Bühler's *Indische Palaeographie*, published in 1896. In respect of the languages used in the inscriptions, we can only say here that they include Sanskṛit, Pāli, some of the Prākṛits, the mixed dialect or dialects, and the older dialects of Kanarese, Marāṭhī, Malayāḷam, Tamiḻ, and Telugu; adding that, though in this detail some of the records offer problems which have still to be solved, they present no substantial initial difficulties to explorers who will use, along with grammars and dictionaries, the more recently and critically edited treatments of the texts and translations. In respect of the diction, we can only observe that the inscriptions were composed sometimes entirely in prose, sometimes entirely in verse, and sometimes in prose and verse mixed. And, in respect of the eras in which so many of the inscriptions were dated, and of the methods according to which the precise dates were stated, we can only refer to certain special works and tables which will be mentioned farther on. Those are technical topics which cannot be handled here. Also, while a sufficient indication must be given of the various purposes to which the inscriptions can be applied, we shall not present here even a summary of the historical and other results obtained from them; those results form the topics of other contributions to this volume.

We have to deal here with the inscriptions from other points of view. We have to explain the nature of them. We have to illustrate the value of them, and show in a general way the ends to which they may be utilized, and establish the necessity for an exhaustive examination of them. And we have to indicate the nature of the work which still remains to be done on them, and to point out certain subsidiary lines of research which ought to be systematically followed up in connexion with them. In leading, as we hope to do, new workers into a field of exploration in which there is a vast amount of important work still to be done, especially in connexion with the more ancient periods, we have to make the way easy for them, by showing them how to avoid the mistakes of previous explorers, and how to direct their own inquiries to the greatest advantage.

II. The Value of the Inscriptions

The value of the inscriptions.

Rich as have been their bequests to us in other lines, the Hindūs have not transmitted to us any historical works which can be accepted as reliable for any early times. And it is almost entirely from a patient examination of the inscriptions, the start in which was made more than a century ago, that our knowledge of the ancient political history of India has been derived. But we are also ultimately dependent on the inscriptions in every other line of Indian research. Hardly any definite dates and identifications can be established except from them. And they regulate everything that we can learn from tradition, literature, coins, art, architecture, or any other source.

While, however, the inscriptions contain the historical and other information which we seek, they were written, engraved, and published, not with the object of presenting that information, but for other purposes which will be made apparent further on; and as a rule it is only incidentally, and as a purely secondary consideration, that they record the details which are so valuable to us. The collection of those details, therefore, is a matter that requires time and patience. The general value of the inscriptions lies mostly in the way in which they all work in, one with another. It follows that our results are, for the most part, obtained only by an examination and combination of large numbers of the epigraphic records; as, for instance, in the process which enabled Professor Kielhorn (see IA, 20. 404 ff.[1]) to dispel the influence of a myth, the Vikrama-legend, which had long dominated certain theories about the history of Sanskṛit literature and other matters, by showing that the so-called Vikrama era, beginning in 58 B.C., was neither established by, nor designedly invented in memory of, any king Vikramāditya who actually flourished at that time[2]. It is not always

[1] For the explanation of the abbreviations used in this chapter, see the list on page 87 f. below.

[2] The legend belongs specially to the Jains. As regards this part of it, Professor Kielhorn has shown that the era of 58 B.C. was known in A.D. 473 and 532-33 as 'the reckoning of the Mālavas,' and in A.D. 879 as 'the Mālava time or era,' and that records of A.D. 738 and 1169 speak of it as 'the years of the Mālava lord or lords.' He has shown that the word *vikrama* is first found coupled with it in a record of A.D. 842 which speaks of 'the time called *vikrama*,' and that we hear for the first time of a prince or king named Vikrama, in connexion with the era, in a poem composed in A.D. 993, the author of which gives its date by saying that he was writing one thousand and fifty years 'after king Vikrama had ascended to the pure dwelling of the immortals.' And he has shown that the first specific mention of the era as having been established by Vikramāditya is in a record of A.D. 1198. He has pointed out that these facts 'would seem to indicate that the connexion of Vikrama with the era grew up gradually, or was an innovation which took centuries to become generally adopted.' And he has put forward the very reasonable opinion that the word *vikrama*, from which the idea of the king Vikrama or Vikramāditya was evolved, most probably came to be connected with the era by the poets, because the years of the reckoning originally began in the autumn, and the autumn was the season for commencing campaigns, and was, in short, the *vikrama-kāla* or 'war-time.'

On the general question, reference may be made to a note by the present writer, in IA, 1901. 3 f. All the results of epigraphic research emphatically endorse Professor Kielhorn's conclusions, and point, as far as we can see at present, to the period between A.D. 842 and 993 as the time during which

that a single inscription, taken by itself, will establish anything of special importance; and we must, at any rate, not make a start in epigraphy with the expectation of achieving a great discovery in the first new record that we examine. It is not every day that we are able to obtain a Rummindēī inscription (EI, 5. 4) which locates at once the birthplace of a Buddha; or a Mandasōr inscription (F.GI, 79, and see introd., 65 ff.) which settles at once the long-disputed question of the epoch of an Indian era, that of the great Gupta kings; or a Takht-i-Bahaī inscription which (see JRAS, 1905. 223 ff.; 1906. 706 ff.) furnishes corroborative evidence of a Christian tradition about an apostle and an Indian king, St. Thomas and Gondophernēs [1].

A. The Absence of Ancient Historical Compilations in India

The absence of ancient historical compilations in India.

It has been said above, that the Hindūs have not bequeathed to us any historical work which can be accepted as reliable for any early times. It is, indeed, very questionable whether the ancient Hindūs ever possessed the true historical sense, in the shape of the faculty of putting together genuine history on broad and critical lines. As we shall see, they could write

the first crude rudiments of the full legend were evolved, or at least were brought into something like a substantial story.

It has further now become clear that that part of the legend which connects certain alien foes with Vikramāditya is ultimately based upon nothing but a confusion (see JRAS, 1905. 643 ff.; 1906. 161, 176) between Saka, Śaka, as the name of a foreign people, and the epigraphic forms Saka, Śaka, = Sakka, Śakka, Sakya, Śakya, Śākya, a 'Buddhist.' That part of it rests, not upon wars between an Indian king and foreign invaders of his country, but upon the rivalry, with varying success, during the first centuries before and after the Christian era, between the Buddhists and the Jains.

The reckoning of 58 B.C. was founded by Kanishka, in the sense that the opening years of it were the years of his reign; it was set going as an era by his successor, who, instead of breaking the reckoning, so started, by introducing another according to his own regnal years, continued it; and it was accepted and perpetuated as an era by the Mālava people, and so was transmitted to posterity by them: see JRAS, 1905. 233; 1906. 979; 1907. 169.

[1] In connexion with this matter it may be added that, whereas the Syriac version of the Acts of St. Thomas mentions a certain Gad as a brother of king Gūdnaphar, Gondophernēs (IA, 1904. 4), there has recently been obtained, from the territory to which the Takht-i-Bahaī inscription belongs, an intaglio (see the *Annual Report of the Archaeological Survey of India* for 1902-3. 167) which bears the Kharōshṭhī legend *Gadasa*, 'of Gada (Gad).' It would be rash to jump to the conclusion that we have here a souvenir of Gad himself, brother of Gondophernēs. But we have evidence, in this new discovery, that the name Gad is at least not purely legendary.

short historical compositions, concise and to the point, but limited in extent. But no evidence of the possession by them of the faculty of dealing with history on general lines has survived to us in the shape of any genuine historical work, deliberately written by them as such, and also accurate and reliable.

The experience of the Arabian writer Albērūnī, in the eleventh century, was, that 'the Hindūs do not pay much attention to the historical order of things, they are very careless in relating the chronological succession of their kings, and when they are pressed for information and are at a loss, not knowing what to say, they invariably take to tale-telling.'[1] And certainly, such attempts as have been made by the Hindūs of more recent times do not display any capabilities from which we might infer that their early ancestors possessed the faculty, even if they did not exercise it.

Early in the last century, there was put together—apparently quite spontaneously, and not in consequence of any lead given by western inquiries—a Kanarese compilation entitled Rājāvalikathe, or 'the story of the succession of kings,' which purports to trace the history of Jainism, especially in connexion with the province of Mysore, on the political history of which, also, it pretends to throw light, from the earliest possible times: the published extracts from this work[2], however, show that it is simply an imaginative production, of the most fanciful kind, based on the wildest legends, to which no value of any sort can be attached for early historical purposes[3]. At apparently some earlier time, as yet not fixed, there was drawn up, in the same part of the country, a Tamiḻ chronicle entitled Koṅgudēśarājākkaḷ[4], or 'the kings of the Koṅgu country,' which purports to give a connected historical account of Mysore from the first century A.D.: but in this case, again, the fanciful nature of the work, and its utter want of reliability for any purposes of early

[1] Sachau's translation of Albērūnī's India, 2. 10.

[2] See EC, 2, Inscriptions at Śravaṇa-Beḷgoḷa, introd. 3 ff., 8 ff., 25 f., 61.

[3] For one illustration of this, see IA, 21. 157; and regarding the apocryphal character of one of the earlier works on which it may be based, the Bhadrabāhucharita, see EI, 4. 23, note 1.

[4] There is an abstract of the contents of this work, by Dowson, in JRAS, 1846. 1 ff.; and a translation, by Taylor, in the Madras *Journal of Literature and Science*, 14, 1847. 1 ff. Burnell condemned the work in his *South-Indian Palaeography*, 1874. 26, note 1; 1878. 33, note 1.

Regarding the 'Chronicle of Toragal,' another document of the same class, but on a smaller scale, produced by the astrologers of Beḷgaum and Manōḷi, see IA, 30, 1901. 201, note 3.

history, are disclosed at once by the very slightest thoughtful examination in the light of present knowledge: for instance, at the outset, not only does it give, as real facts, the fictitious pedigree and history with which we are familiar from the spurious copperplate records of the Western Gaṅga series, but also (see EI, 3. 170), before the first of the fictitious Gaṅga kings, it places in the period A.D. 82 to 178, and before that time, some of the Rāshṭrakūṭa kings whose dates really lay between A.D. 675 and 956. Notices of other chronicles, relating, for instance, to the Chōḷa, Pallava, and Pāṇḍya territories and to the Teliṅgāna country, are to be found in Professor H. H. Wilson's *Descriptive Catalogue of the Mackenzie Collection*. These have, perhaps, not yet been criticized in detail. But a perusal of the notices discloses features very similar to those of the Rājāvalikathe and the Koṅgudēśa-rājākkaḷ. And, though they may be of some use in the geographical line of inquiry, we have no prima-facie reason to expect to find in these works, also, anything of the slightest historical value for early days.

B. Pedigrees and Successions

Pedigrees and successions.

Yet there were once, undoubtedly, genuine materials in abundance, from which histories of the most valuable kind might have been compiled in ancient times.

In the first place, we, who have lived in India, know how, in that country, pedigrees are always forthcoming, even in the present day, to an extent that is unknown in western lands. Among families connected in any way hereditarily with the administration, even the Gauḍas or Pāṭīls (the village headmen) and the Kuḷkarṇīs (the accountants) can always bring forward, whenever there is any inquiry into their *watans* or rights and privileges, or any dispute among themselves, genealogical tables, unquestionably not altogether unauthentic, which exhibit the most complicated ramifications of their houses, and often go back for two or three centuries; and even the death of an ordinary cultivator usually results in the production of a similar table, though of more limited scope, in the inquiry that is held to determine his heirs. Every *maṭha* or religious college of any importance preserves the succession of its heads. And among the Jains we have the Paṭṭāvalis or successions of pontiffs, for a full and lucid notice of some of which we are indebted to Dr. Hoernle (IA, 20. 341; 21. 57)[1]. They purport to run

[1] For others, see Klatt in IA, 11. 245, 251; Peterson's *Second Report on*

back to even the death of the last Tīrthaṁkara Vardhamāna-Mahāvīra in (let us say) 527 B.C.; and, though the earlier portions of them were probably put together in their present form not before the ninth century A.D. (because they exhibit the Vikrama-legend; see page 4 above, and note 2) and with results that are capable of considerable adjustment, they are, no doubt, based upon more ancient and correct lists that were then extant.

The preservation of pedigrees and successions has evidently been a national characteristic for many centuries. And we cannot doubt that considerable attention was paid to the matter in connexion with the royal families, and that Vaṁśāvalis or Rājāvalis, lists of the lineal successions of kings, were compiled and kept from very early times. In fact, the matter is not one of speculation, but is capable of proof. We distinctly recognize the use of such Vaṁśāvalis, giving the relationships and successions of kings, but no chronological details beyond the record of the total duration of each reign, with occasionally a coronation-date recorded in an era, in the copperplate records. We trace them, for instance, in the introductory passages of the grants of the Eastern Chalukya series (see, e.g., IA, 14. 55; H.SII, 1. 36; EI, 5. 131; 7. 177), which, from the period A.D. 918 to 925 onwards, name the successive kings, beginning with the founder of the line who reigned three centuries before that time, but do not put forward more than the length of the reign of each of them; and, from certain differences in the figures for some of the reigns, we recognize that there were varying recensions of those Vaṁśāvalis. And we trace the use of Vaṁśāvalis again in the similar records of the Eastern Gaṅgas of Kaliṅga, which, from A.D. 1058 onwards (see EI, 4. 183), give the same details about the kings of that line with effect from about A.D. 890, and one of which, issued in A.D. 1296 (JASB, 65, 1896. 229), includes a coronation-date of A.D. 1141 or 1142.

There is other proof also[1]. There has been brought to light from Nēpāl a long Vaṁśāvali (IA, 13. 411), which purports to give an unbroken list of the rulers of that country, with

Sanskṛit MSS., 89, 163; and Bhandarkar's *Report on Sanskṛit MSS.* for 1883-84. 14, 319.

[1] Kalhaṇa, writing the Rājataraṁgiṇī in A.D. 1148-49, mentions lists of kings of Kashmīr which had been put together by Kshēmēndra and Hēlārāja (compare page 16 below). But we do not quote these as proof of our present point; because they were compilations, not original lists prepared under the dynasties to which they referred.

the lengths of their reigns and an occasional landmark in the shape of the date of an accession stated in an era, back from A.D. 1768 to even so fabulous an antiquity as six or seven centuries before the commencement of the Kali age in 3102 B.C. It contains gross mistakes in chronology: for instance, it places in 101 to 34 B.C. Aṁśuvarman, of the Ṭhākurī dynasty, who, we know, was ruling in A.D. 635 and 649 or 650 (F.GI, introd., 189); and, partly through committing one of the usual leading faults of Hindū compilations, namely, of treating contemporaneous dynasties as successive dynasties, it places about the end of the seventh century B.C. a certain Vṛishadēva, of the Sūryavaṁśi or Lichchhavi dynasty, who, we know, was a contemporary of Aṁśuvarman. And, as was pointed out by Pandit Bhagwanlal Indraji, who brought the full Vaṁśāvali to notice critically, 'it possesses no value whatever as a whole,' and 'no single one of its several portions is free from the most serious errors,' and it is useless for reconstructing the earlier history of Nēpāl, even by adjustment with respect to any names and dates that are known from other sources. But, in connexion with the above-mentioned Vṛishadēva, and in spite of the error in respect of his date, it teaches one thing which is of use. From him, whom it places No. 18 in the Sūryavaṁśi dynasty, to Vasantadēva, No. 23, it gives correctly a list of six successive names, which we have verified from epigraphic records. It allots to each of these rulers, it is true, a length of reign which not only is impossible in itself, but also is disproved in one case at least by the inscriptions. But the fact remains, that the names are given correctly and in the right order. This short list was certainly not based on some ancient charter read by the original compiler of this portion of the Vaṁśāvali. What would have happened, if that had been the case, is suggested plainly enough by the Konnūr inscription from the Dhārwār District (EI, 6. 25), which purports to be the reproduction of a charter, dated A.D. 860, of the time of the Rāshṭrakūṭa king Amōghavarsha I. Here, we have a record on stone, which says that it was embodied in that shape in accordance with a copperplate charter that was read and explained by a certain Jain teacher named Vīranandin, son of Mēghachandra. Partly from the characters of the record, and partly from the established fact that Mēghachandra died A.D. 1115, we know that this record was not put on the stone before the twelfth century A.D. We do not dispute the alleged fact that Vīranandin drafted the stone record from some ancient charter on copper. But we find either that he could not read that charter correctly, or that he did not take the trouble to interpret it aright; for, not only has he misstated the relationships of some of the Rāshṭrakūṭa kings whom the stone version does mention, and omitted others whom it ought to have included, but also—probably from a wrong interpretation of some verse which we have not as yet found in a genuine record—he has placed at the head of the Rāshṭrakūṭa genealogy a purely fictitious person, whom he has called Prichchhakarāja. If the list from Vṛishadēva to Vasantadēva in the Nēpāl Vaṁśāvali had been put together in the same way from some ancient deed, the compiler of that part of the document would undoubtedly have committed some similar mistakes. We have no hesitation in saying that he took these six names from some genuine early Vaṁśāvali, accessible to him, which had survived from the time of the rulers to whom it referred; and probably the duration of the reigns was given correctly by him, and was falsified subsequently by some later compiler to suit his own scheme of the whole chronology.

The Bower Manuscript has proved to us that, under favourable conditions, a document written on even so frail a material as birch-bark can survive for fourteen centuries. This manuscript was obtained in Kashgaria, on the north of Kashmīr, through excavations at 'the foot of one of the curious old erections, of which several are to be found in the Kuchar district.' It was secured and brought to notice by Lieutenant Bower (see JASB, 59, 1890. proceedings, 221), from whom it derives its name. And Dr. Hoernle has shown (IA, 21. 37), by a comparison of its characters with those of epigraphic records, that in it we have a veritable original document, which is a relic that has come down to us from the period A.D. 400 to 450. With this instance before us, we may not unreasonably hope that an exploration of some buried city, or even of one or other of the numerous private collections of ancient manuscripts that still remain to be examined, may some day result in the discovery of some of the early and authentic Vaṁśāvalis.

Meanwhile, we have to be very cautious in accepting what we do obtain in this line. We have before us the example, not only of the Nēpāl Vaṁśāvali, but also of some Vaṁśāvalis from Orissa, which do not indeed pretend to quite such fabulous antiquity, but which nevertheless purport to present an unbroken list of the kings of that province back from A.D. 1871 to the commencement of the Kali age in 3102 B.C., with the length of the reign of each, and with certain specified dates as epochs.

And the results put forward by them, and by the palm-leaf archives of the temple of Jagannātha at Purī, have been supposed to give at any rate certain definite and reliable landmarks in the early history. But an examination of them and of the archives (see EI, 3. 334 ff.) has shown that, for at least the period anterior to about A.D. 1100, they are utterly fanciful and misleading, and that they were devised, chiefly from imagination, simply to magnify the antiquity and importance of the temple of Jagannātha and of all its surroundings and connexions. These local annals are not correct even in respect of so radical a point as the building of that temple. They attribute it to a king Anaṅgabhīma, whom they would place A.D. 1175 to 1202; whereas we know from the epigraphic records that it was built by a predecessor of his, Anantavarma-Chōḍagaṅga-Gaṅgēśvara, in the period A.D. 1075 to 1141 or 1142. Further, they actually divide this latter king into two persons, Chōḍagaṅga and Gaṅgēśvara, to whom they would allot the periods A.D. 1132 to 1152 and 1152 to 1166. For the period anterior to him, they do not incorporate any ancient and authentic lists of rulers, but simply bring forward, amongst a host of fabulous names, a few historic kings, some of them not even connected with Orissa at all, whose dates they grossly misplace. Thus these records, again, are absolutely worthless for any purposes of ancient history.

C. Official Records

In the genuine early Vaṁśāvalis, materials must long have been extant, which could have been turned to most valuable account, if only for the bare outlines of political history. But there were plainly more ample materials than these. Of course, the elaborate routine of modern times had not been devised. Still, with the great advance towards civilization which the Hindūs had made even in the fourth century B.C., and with the careful and detailed system of administration which is disclosed by the inscriptional remains, there must have been, from early times, a fairly extensive system of official records. In any such state of advancement there are certain precautions and arrangements, indicated by common sense, which would inevitably be adopted. Copies of important orders issued must be kept on record in the issuing office, as a reminder to make sure that instructions given are duly and fully carried out; and orders received must be filed in the receiving office, to be produced in justification of any particular measures taken in giving effect to them. The specific terms of treaties and alliances must be reduced to writing; and copies must be kept

Official records.

for reference by each of the contracting parties. Diaries of some kind must be kept by local governors, from which to prepare from time to time the periodical reports on their administration. A record must be kept, on both sides, of tribute paid by the great feudatory nobles and received by the paramount sovereign. And, even under a system of farming the revenues, accounts of some kind must be framed, of the proceeds of provincial customs and taxes and of village revenues, and of the expenditure incurred on the collection of them.

Notes of all such matters must have been preserved in some form or another, in all the various offices. But it is probable that they were kept in the shape of general day-books, something like the Diaries of the Pēshwās of the eighteenth century[1], dealing with all matters mixed, rather than according to any system of separate ledgers and files for each branch of business. Except on the hypothesis of such a system of day-books, it is difficult to account for the manner in which, for instance, the date of a record of A.D. 1008 at Tanjore (H.SII, 3. 14) cites the 124th and 143rd days of the twenty-fourth year of the Chōḷa king Rājarāja I, and the date of a record of A.D. 1113 at Tiruvārūr in the Tanjore district (EI, 4. 73) cites the 340th day of the fifth year of the reign of his descendant Vikrama-Chōḷadēva; for such details to be cited conveniently there must have been available some such books, in which the days were entered and numbered, and the events of them were posted up, as they ran[2].

D. Dynastic Archives and Chronicles

Dynastic archives and chronicles.

In such day-books and other records, valuable items of historical information would abound. The compilation, however, of any general history from them would, no doubt, be

[1] For an indication of the nature of these Diaries, reference may be made to the extracts relating to political matters from the Rōjniśī or Journal of the Mahārāja Śāhu of Sātārā from A.D. 1713–14 to 1734-35, published at Poona in or about 1900. Some of the Pēshwās' Diaries themselves have, it is believed, been published since then.

[2] A rather curious instance of citing the days is furnished by the Tiruppūvanam grant of the Pāṇḍya king Jaṭāvarma-Kulaśēkhara (IA, 20. 288), which mentions the 4,360th day of his thirteenth year. We can hardly imagine that the numbering of the days had run on from the first day of the reign up to that high number. And we understand that, as suggested (loc. cit., 289), the writer took the fortieth day of the thirteenth year, and, for some reason or other, added it to 360 × 12 = 4,320 as the total number of the days of the preceding twelve years.

a somewhat complicated and laborious matter. But there were, plainly, other materials of a more concise kind, that might have been used with great facility, in the shape of dynastic archives and chronicles, which, in some cases at least, survived for a considerable time after the disappearance of the dynasties to which they belonged, and from which comprehensive and very valuable accounts might easily have been put together.

It can only have been from ancient archives, of considerable fullness of detail, which had fallen into their own hands, that the Western Chālukya kings of Kalyāṇi (A.D. 973 to 1189) derived the knowledge that they possessed, and exhibited in some of their records, of the earlier Chalukya dynasty of Bādāmi (about A.D. 550 to 757)—separated from themselves by an interval of more than two centuries, during which an extraneous dynasty possessed the sovereignty—from which they claimed to be descended. This is pointedly illustrated by the mention, in the Kauthēṁ plates of A.D. 1009 (IA, 16. 15), of Maṅgalēśa, who was not in the direct line of descent, and therefore might easily have been lost sight of in a mere Vaṁśāvali, and by the preservation, in the same record, among certain other details for which tradition alone, or a mere list of kings, would not account, of the memory of the conquest by him of the territory of Rēvatidvīpa, and by the way in which the record seeks to obliterate his attempt to break the direct and rightful senior line of succession in favour of transmitting the crown to his own son, by representing him as simply a regent during the minority of his nephew Pulakēśin II, to whom, it says, he eventually restored the throne in pious accordance with the custom and laws of the Chalukya kings. And the Śilāhāra princes of the Southern Koṅkaṇ must have kept a careful record of their paramount sovereigns, the Rāshṭrakūṭas (A.D. 754 to 973), as well as of themselves, to account for the statement about the rise of their own family under Kṛishṇa I. in the period between A.D. 878 and 912, and for the full account of the Rāshṭrakūṭa genealogy, as well as of their own pedigree, that is given in the Khārēpāṭaṇ plates of A.D. 1008 (EI, 3. 293), issued by the Śilāhāra Raṭṭarāja in the time of the Western Chālukya king Iṛivabeḍaṅga-Satyāśraya.

These cases indicate distinctly the compilation and survival of dynastic chronicles, which were doubtless carried on chapter by chapter after the death of each successive king or prince. And we can actually recognize the copy of a chapter, or of the draft of the beginning of a chapter, of such a chronicle, compiled most probably from day-books or other such sources, in the Hāthigumphā cave-inscription, of 156–55 B.C. if it is really dated in the 165th year of the time of the Maurya kings (C.IA, plate 17; Sixth Oriental Congress, 3. 135), which gives a succinct account of the career of king Khāravēla of Kaliṅga from his birth to the thirteenth year of his reign: it tells us that he spent fifteen years in princely sports; that for nine years he enjoyed power as Yuvarāja or heir-apparent and appointed successor; and that he was crowned to the succession at the end of his twenty-fourth year; and then it briefly enumerates, year by year, the principal events of his reign, and certain large items of expenditure on public works and charity, as far as the thirteenth year. In this department, again, we may hope that future explorations will result in discoveries of a particularly interesting kind.

E. The Purāṇas

The Purāṇas. Those materials did not remain altogether unutilized. We can trace a use of at least Vaṁśāvalis in the historical chapters given in some of the Purāṇas, which do certainly indicate a desire on the part of the ancient Hindūs not to ignore general history altogether, and are clearly based upon ancient archives which had survived in a more or less complete shape and were somehow or other accessible to the composers of those works, or upon some prototype which had been so based.

At the same time it is not very much, in the way of reliable history, that we gather from these chapters in the Purāṇas. In the first place, some of the necessary materials were apparently not available to the authors, and some of the dynasties are omitted altogether. For instance, the Purāṇas do not include (at any rate with any clearness) any references to the line established in Northern India by Kanishka, who, in doing that, founded the so-called Vikrama era commencing in 58 B.C. (see page 4 above, and note 2), or to the line established in Western India by that king of Kāṭhiāwār and Ujjain, apparently of Pahlava, Parthian, extraction, who thereby founded the so-called Śaka era of A.D. 78. They mention the great dynasty of the Guptas (A.D. 320 to about 530) in merely a vague manner, without individual names, as kings reigning over Sākēta and the Magadha country and along the Ganges as far as Prayāga (Allahābād)—a description which can only apply to the actual rise of the Gupta power under Chandragupta I. (A.D. 320 to about 335). And with this statement about the Guptas—whom (by the way) they would place more than three centuries ahead of the present day—they close their treatment of the dynasties: no later history is found in them. In the second place, the authors did not think it worth their while to give us any fixed points, in the shape of dates recorded in any of the Hindū eras, to which we might refer their statements. Thirdly, they are by no means in exact agreement with each other in respect of the details which they give regarding the lengths of individual reigns or even the duration of each dynasty. In the fourth place, even allowing for corruption by successive copyists, it seems plain that—be the cause what it may; sometimes, perhaps, inability to decipher ancient characters—they have not always given us even the names of their kings with accuracy: compare, for instance, the Purāṇic lists of the Andhrabhṛityas with each other, and still more with such information about those kings as we have obtained from the epigraphic records. Finally, the chronological results of these chapters show that here, again, the authors committed the fault of treating contemporaneous dynasties as successive: thus (to take only a part of the whole list), from the beginning of the Mauryas to the end of the Kailakila-Yavanas the Purāṇas give us a total period of more than 2,500 years; apply this to 320 B.C. as the initial year of the first Maurya king Chandragupta (see JRAS, 1906. 984 f.), and we have the end of the Kailakila-Yavanas about A.D. 2200, some three centuries in the future from even the present time; and we have to place after that a variety of other rulers, including the Guptas (A.D. 320 to about 530), who, the same works say, followed the Kailakila-Yavanas.

In short, in the historical chapters of the Purāṇas the treatment of their subject is sketchy and meagre, and the details are discrepant. We may utilize these chapters to a certain extent for general purposes, if we discriminate so as to place synchronously in different territories some of the dynasties which they exhibit as ruling successively over the same dominions. But we cannot apply them more precisely without appreciably more corroboration than has as yet been obtained from epigraphic and numismatic sources.

F. The Rājataraṁgiṇī

The only other indication, that has survived from any antiquity, of an attempt on the part of the Hindūs to put together anything in the shape of a general history, is the Rājataraṁgiṇī, **The Rājataraṁgiṇī.**

on the first eight cantos of which Kalhaṇa was engaged in A.D. 1148–49.

Kalhaṇa mentions certain previous writers: Suvrata, whose work (he says) was made difficult by misplaced learning; Kshēmēndra, who drew up a list of kings, of which, however (he says) no part is free from mistakes; Nīlamuni, who wrote the Nīlamata-Purāṇa; Hēlārāja, who composed a list of kings in 12,000 verses; Padmamihira; and Chhavillākara. His own work, he tells us, was based on eleven collections of Rājakathās or 'stories about kings,'[1] and on the work of Nīlamuni. He says he sought to remove all errors by consulting charters issued by ancient kings, and laudatory inscriptions on stones, and manuscripts. And he has presented us with a detailed account of Kashmīr, including occasional items of external history, which purports to go back to 2448 B.C., and has given us the alleged exact details of the length of the reign of each successive king from 1182 B.C. onwards.

We may expect to find Kalhaṇa fairly correct for his own time, and for the preceding century or so. But an examination of the details of his work quickly exposes its imaginative character, and its unreliability for any earlier period. It places towards the close of the period 2448 to 1182 B.C. the great Maurya king Aśōka, whose real initial date, as determined by his *abhishēka* or anointment to the sovereignty, was 264 B.C. (see JRAS, 1906. 985 f.). It places in 704 to 634 B.C. Mihirakula, the great foreign invader of India, whose real period was closely about A.D. 530 (F.GI, introd. 11). It places about seven centuries after Mihirakula a Tōramāṇa, the original of whom can hardly be any other than Tōramāṇa the father of Mihirakula. And, though Kalhaṇa could put forward such exact details as four years, nine months, and one day for the duration of the reign of Mātṛigupta (A.D. 106 to 111, as placed by him), he was obliged to allot to Raṇāditya I. a reign of three centuries (A.D. 222 to 522), simply in order to save his own chronology.

[1] Compare, especially as helping to illustrate how fictitious matter might come to be introduced into such stories and to be disseminated by them, the discourse about religion, and the recital of the praises of ancient and recent devotees of Śiva, in which Sōmēśvara IV. and his commander-in-chief indulged on a certain occasion (EI, 5. 258; see also ibid. 233, for another instance of a *dharmaprasaṅga* or talk about religion between village officials).

G. General Literature and Historical Romances

General literature and historical romances.

With those exceptions, namely, the historical chapters of the Purāṇas and the Rājataraṁgiṇī, the ancient Hindūs seem to have never made any real attempt to deal with history on general lines. They have left us to gather what we can from their ordinary literary works, into which they have occasionally introduced historical matter, but, as can clearly be seen, only as an incidental detail of quite secondary and subordinate importance.

In the body of their literature, the Hindūs do not help us much. The plots of some of the plays, the classical poems, and the collections of imaginative stories, were woven round historic names, both of persons and of places. But it is seldom, except in the geographical line, that such allusions can be put to any practical use. They help us to locate places, and to fix the limits of countries. For instance, we know, from other sources, that the ancient Tāmaliptī is the modern Tamlūk in the Midnapūr District; and thus an incidental statement of the Daśakumāracharita, that Tāmaliptī was in the Suhma country[1], gives us a more precise indication than is obtainable elsewhere as to the exact part of Bengal that was known by the name of Suhma. So, also, for another part of Bengal, the statement in the Dīgha-Nikāya, 1. 111; 2. 235, that Champā, which is known to be represented by a village which forms the western part of the town of Bhāgalpūr, was in Aṅga, gives us a similar indication as to the exact position of the Aṅga country. And they help us to establish the antiquity of places: thus, we know, from the Aihoḷe inscription of the time of Pulakēśin II, that the celebrated poet Kālidāsa flourished before A.D. 634; and so the mention by him, in the Raghuvaṁśa, 8. 33, of Gōkarṇa, in the North Kanara District, carries back the existence of that place, as a famous Śaiva site, to at least the beginning of the seventh century A.D. In the historical line, however, the allusions teach us little, if anything. The works do not give dates for what is told in them: and naturally enough: the similar productions of other countries, also, do not aim at being historical records, and at including chronological details. The works in question are of use, historically, only when the

[1] The name is actually presented as Dāmalipta in the text, in the beginning of the sixth chapter, both in Wilson's edition and in Peterson's. There is, however, no question about that form being only a variant of the better known Tāmaliptī.

date of an author happens to be known, and we are enabled thereby to fix a latest possible limit for an historic name, mentioned by him, for which we have otherwise no specific date at all.

There are, indeed, a few compositions which put forward certain distinct historical pretensions, but which cannot, in truth, be taken as anything more serious than historical romances.

In Sanskṛit, we have in prose the Harshacharita of Bāṇa, and in verse the Vikramāṅkadēvacharita of Bilhaṇa. The first deals with the achievements or career of the great northern king Harsha, Harshadēva, or Harshavardhana, of Ṭhāṇēsar and Kanauj (A.D. 605–6 to about 648); and the second deals, in the same way, with an equally great southern king of later times, the Western Chālukya Vikramāditya VI, of Kalyāṇi (A.D. 1076 to 1126). Thus they both aim at being historical chronicles of those two periods. But they do not present the plain straightforward language of sober common sense. They imitate the classical poems, with all their elaboration of diction, metaphor, and imagery. They weave into their stories mythical and supernatural matter of the most fanciful kind. And they give us some charming reading in the poetical line. But they offer us not much beyond that. The historical information contained in the Harshacharita might be summed up very briefly. That in the Vikramāṅkadēvacharita is more extensive; mixed up, on the other hand, with more imaginative matter than is found in Bāṇa's work. But neither author has given us a date for anything that is mentioned by him. We do not blame them for this: the authors of the modern European historical novels rarely give dates; and, when they do, we should hardly accept their statements for quotation without verification. We only remark that no dates are given. Bāṇa, for instance, tells us that Harshavardhana was born 'in the month Jyaishṭha, on the twelfth day of the dark fortnight, when the moon was standing in the Pleiades, just after the twilight time, when the young night had begun to climb;'[1] but he has not given us any statement as to the year. And Bilhaṇa tells us that, when Vikramāditya was born, 'flowers fell from the sky, Indra's drum resounded, and the gods rejoiced in heaven' (IA, 5. 318); but he does not even name the month and day. Neither

[1] Translation by Cowell and Thomas, 109; but with a correction, in respect of the allusion to the Pleiades, from the text, Kashmīr edition, 284.

author has given us even his own date. And so, if Harsha-vardhana and Vikramāditya were not known from more exact sources of a different kind, we should not even know to what period to refer the poets and their patrons.

In the same category we must place the Tamil historical poems, the Kaḷavaḷi, the Kaliṅgattu-Paraṇi, and the Vikrama-Chōḷan-Ulā, for our introduction to which we are indebted to Mr. V. Kanakasabhai Pillai (IA, 18. 259; 19. 329; 22. 141). In these, again, there is a great deal of charming reading, and much of interest, and a good deal of importance. But here, also, there are no dates, and therefore no means in the works themselves for determining the periods to which they belong.

These works, the dramas, the classical poems, the imaginative stories, and the historical romances, and so also the Buddhist writings both Sanskṛit and Pāli, are invaluable for the study of manners and customs, trade and commerce, methods and routes of communication, geographical hints, and the details of domestic, social, public, and religious life. They would furnish excellent materials for articles such as those which the Rev. T. Foulkes has given us, from the Buddhist works, on the Deccan in the time of Gautama-Buddha (IA, 16. 1 ff., 49 ff.). And they supplement the epigraphic records admirably. But that is all they do. And, even in respect of the results which we do obtain from such sources, we must always remember that the ancient Hindū writers were not archaeologists, and that, consequently, the results are liable to be for the times in which the writers wrote, rather than for the times to which their works refer.

H. Introductions and Colophons of Literary Works

Introductions and colophons of literary works.

It is only in the introductions and colophons of their literary works, for a knowledge of which we are indebted largely to the detailed reports of Professor Peterson and of Dr. Bhandarkar on Sanskṛit manuscripts, that the Hindūs have thought it worth their while to give us any dates to accompany such historical details as they put forward. Here, the dates are useful enough. But we find that the historical matter is introduced only incidentally, to magnify the importance of the authors themselves rather than of their patrons, and is not handled with any particular care and fullness. As typical illustrations, we take the following cases.

Sōmadēva tells us, in the colophon of his Yaśastilaka [1], that he finished that work in the month Chaitra, the Śaka year 881

[1] Peterson's *Second Report*, 47.

expired, falling in A.D. 959, during the rule of a Chālukya prince who was the eldest son of Arikēsarin and was a feudatory of a king Kṛishṇarājadēva. But he does not take the trouble to tell us the name of the prince, presumably his immediate patron, or to state the family or even the parentage of the king, or to indicate the territory of either the sovereign or his vassal. In this case, as it happens, we learn more about the family of the prince from the Vikramārjunavijaya or Pampa-Bhārata of Pampa, who, writing A.D. 941–42, mentions as his patron the aforesaid Arikēsarin, and gives his pedigree for seven preceding generations, with apparently a tolerably definite hint as to the part of the country to which he belonged[1]. As regards the king Kṛishṇarājadēva, we knew, from the epigraphic records, the Rāshṭrakūṭa king Kṛishṇa III, for whom we had dates in A.D. 940 and 956. And, there being no extraneous objections, we did not hesitate to identify Sōmadēva's Kṛishṇarājadēva with this Kṛishṇa III, and to extend the reign of the latter to A.D. 959, even before obtaining for him a later epigraphic date in A.D. 961 (see EI, 6. 180). In this way, Sōmadēva's literary reference usefully supplemented the inscriptions. But it teaches us, in itself, little enough. And, by the way, he might plainly have told us even a good deal more than he has. The preamble of the letter issued by his hero king Yaśōdhara[2], particularly in its introduction of the titles 'supreme lord of the town Padmāvatīpura, lord of the mountain Kanakagiri, and owner of the Kailāsa-crest,' as well as in other details, is no mere ordinary epistle, but is an imitation of the formal preamble of a grant; from which we gather that Sōmadēva had access to official papers, and used one of the drafts kept on hand for preparing charters of grants.

Take, again, the case of Jahlaṇa. In the introduction to his Subhāshitamuktāvali, written in the period A.D. 1247 to 1260[3], he states carefully the relationships in his own pedigree, but omits to state them in the case of the Dēvagiri-Yādava kings Bhillama, Siṅghaṇa, and Kṛishṇa, and their ancestor Mallugi, whom he mentions.

Take, finally, the case of Hēmādri. Writing in the period A.D. 1260 to 1271, in the time of the Dēvagiri-Yādava king Mahādēva, under whom, as also under his successor Rāmachandra, he held the post of Śrīkaraṇādhipa or super-

[1] Rice's Pampa-Bhārata, canto 1, verses 15 to 42.

[2] Peterson's *Second Report*, 39.

[3] Bhandarkar's *Report* for 1887–88 to 1890–91. notices, 7.

intendent of the business connected with the drawing up of documents, he aimed, in the introduction to his Vratakhaṇḍa[1], at giving the full pedigree, with incidental historical items, of that branch of the Yādavas from even Purāṇic times. In spite, however, of the free access that he must have had to the chronicles and official records of the family within the historical period, he has omitted, several times, to state the exact relationships of the successive members of the family; he has apparently passed over altogether one of them, Sēuṇadēva, whose existence is established by an epigraphic record; and, as tested by an inscription of A.D. 1191 at Gadag (EI, 3. 216; and see F.DKD, 516), he has suggested an altogether wrong inference regarding the parentage of Bhillama, the first paramount king in the family, within only a century before the time at which he was writing.

I. The Inscriptions

The dates which are given in the introductions and colophons of the literary works, in connexion with the composition of those works, may of course be accepted as reliable; and any genealogical and historical items put forward in the same places ought to be correct for a few preceding generations. But it would be a very extraordinary and imperfect history of India that we should put together from such references, and from the Purāṇas, the Rājataraṁgiṇī, the historical romances, the general body of the literature, such Vaṁśāvalis as have been obtained from Orissa and Nēpāl, and the few items of alleged history that are incidentally given in the Paṭṭāvalis. The inscriptions.

We should doubtless recognize that the successions of kings given for India itself by the Purāṇas, for Kashmīr by the Rājataraṁgiṇī, and for Nēpāl by the Vaṁśāvali, should be taken as separate successions, in territories the histories of which must be treated separately. We should not know exactly what conclusion to arrive at in respect of the annals of Orissa, which is a province of India itself. But, having regard to the preposterous duration allotted to each of the reigns from 3102 to 58 B.C., we should doubtless decide that all memory of the true history of that period had been lost in Orissa, and that from the next fixed point, A.D. 78, Orissa was an independent province with a history and a line of kings of its own. We could scarcely fail to detect the occurrence, in the Purāṇas, the Rājataraṁgiṇī, and the Nēpāl

[1] Bhandarkar's text in the *Gazetteer of the Bombay Presidency*, i, part 2. 268.

Vaṁśāvali, of one particular name, that of Aśōka, which ought to establish a definite synchronous point in the histories of the three countries. We should not be able to deduce the date of Aśōka from the Purāṇas. But we should find that the Rājataraṁgiṇī would place him somewhere about 1260 B.C. We should find, indeed, that the Nēpāl Vaṁśāvali would place him, roughly, about 2600 B.C. As, however, that list does not mention him as a ruler of Nēpāl, but only as a visitor to the country, we should probably infer a mistake in that account, and prefer to select the date of 1260 B.C. And then we should set about arranging the succession of the kings of India itself, from the Purāṇas, with 1260 B.C. for the approximate date of the accession of Aśōka as our starting-point[1].

We should then examine the other available sources of information. And probably we should first note, from the Jain Paṭṭāvalis, the king Vanarāja, who is said to have founded Aṇhilwāḍ, in Gujarāt, in A.D. 746 (IA, 11. 253); and we should obtain the alleged succession at Aṇhilwāḍ after him, with an initial date for each king, to A.D. 1304, from the Pravachanaparīkshā of Dharmasāgara[2]. From the literary works we should obtain a few names, with fixed dates, such as the following. Jinasēna tells us (see EI, 6. 195), in the Jain Harivaṁśa, in connexion with the date of that work, that in A.D. 783–84 there were reigning—in various directions determined with reference to a town named Vardhamānapura, which is to be identified with the modern Waḍhwāṇ in the Jhālāvāḍ division of Kāṭhiāwār—in the north, Indrāyudha; in the south, Śrīvallabha; in the east, Vatsarāja, king of Avanti (Ujjain); in the west, Varāha or Jayavarāha, in the territory of the Sauryas. And from the Channabasavapurāṇa we should have (but, in this case, falsely; because his real date was A.D. 1156 to 1167) a king Bijjala reigning at Kalyāṇi, in the Nizam's Dominions, contemporaneously with them. Guṇabhadra gives us, in recording the completion of his Uttarapurāṇa (see IA, 12. 217), a king Akālavarsha, with the date of A.D. 897. Pampa gives us (see page 20 above) a Chālukya prince Arikēsarin, with the date of A.D. 941, with his pedigree for seven generations, and with, apparently, a hint that he was ruling the territory round the modern Lakshmēshwar in the Dhārwār District. Sōmadēva gives us

[1] A beginning was actually made, in almost the manner suggested above, by Sir William Jones; see his dissertation on the Chronology of the Hindūs written in 1788 (AR, 2. 111, reprint of 1799). But he took a different starting-point, which he fixed in a different way.

[2] Bhandarkar's *Report* for 1883–84. 150, 456.

(see page 20 above) a king Kṛishṇa, with the date of A.D. 959. Ranna gives us[1] a king Āhavamalla, reigning in A.D. 983. A later Sōmadēva gives us (IA, 10. 75) a Bhōja, ruling in the Kōlhāpūr territory in A.D. 1205. And Jñānēśvara gives us[2] a Rāmachandra, reigning in A.D. 1290; while another work (see IA, 21. 51) gives a date for the same king in A.D. 1297, and shows that the Koṅkaṇ was a part of his dominions.

In the way of definite names with uncertain dates, we should have from Jahlaṇa (see page 20 above) another king Kṛishṇa, with his predecessors Mallugi, Bhillama, and Siṅghaṇa, whom we could not place in any particular period from his information alone. And we should have from Hēmādri (see page 20 f. above) a much longer list, in which we should recognize the same names, without, however, here again the means of referring them to any particular period. We should probably obtain the right clue here from the fact that Hēmādri elsewhere mentions, as the successor of his king Mahādēva, a Rāmachandra who, we should guess, ought to be identified with the Rāmachandra of A.D. 1290 and 1297. But in the case of Bāṇa's Harsha (Harshavardhana) and Bilhaṇa's Vikramāditya, we should in all probability go completely wrong: the temptation would be almost irresistible to identify Vikramāditya either with a Vikramāditya who is mentioned in the Rājataraṁgiṇī, 2. 5, 6, as a contemporary of Pratāpāditya of Kashmīr in the asserted period 180 to 148 B.C., or else with the Vikramāditya of Ujjain of the Vikrama-legend (see page 4 above, and note 2), who is supposed according to one version to have died, according to another to have begun to reign, in 58 B.C., and to identify Harsha with a certain Harsha-Vikramāditya, king of Ujjain, who is mentioned in the Rājataraṁgiṇī, 3. 125 ff., as a contemporary of Hiraṇya and Mātṛigupta of Kashmīr in the asserted period A.D. 76 to 111.

We should look in vain in the Purāṇas for any of the names obtained from the literature and the Paṭṭāvalis. But we should, to the best of our ability, work those names, and the dates connected with them, into the list obtained from the Purāṇas and in continuation of it. And we should possibly be working into it also some quite modern inventions, such as those of the bards of Kāṭhiāwār (see F.GI, introd., 49), which were at one time supposed to be 'old-world tales,' but which really sprang into existence some quarter of a century ago, and owe their

[1] Rice's Karṇāṭakaśabdānuśāsanam, introd., 28.
[2] See *Gazetteer of the Bombay Presidency*, i, part 2. 250.

origin only to certain modern speculations which had found their way to the bards through an educational treatise.

In this way we should build up a chronological list of the rulers of India, and of some of its provinces, with 1260 B.C. as a starting-point. Then, sooner or later, we should be met by the discovery that Chandragupta, the grandfather of Aśōka, was known to the Greeks as Sandrokottos, and that his initial date is fixed very closely about 320 B.C. by the Greek writers. We should thus learn that Aśōka could not be placed before about 265 B.C.[1]. All the early part of our arrangements would be upset by a thousand years. And the subject would become a maze of bewilderment, confusion, and speculation, to be approached afresh from an entirely new point of view.

Fortunately, the discovery about Chandragupta was made and announced in 1793 by Sir William Jones[2], before speculation into the ancient history of India had gone very far; and, fortunately, a few of the inscriptions had already begun to come to notice. From that time, more and more attention was paid to them; particularly from the time when they were taken in hand by Mr. James Prinsep, who first succeeded in deciphering the records of Aśōka, and, in that and other ways, laid the real foundations of the whole superstructure that has been subsequently reared up. And it is with relief that we turn to the inscriptions, and lay aside any further consideration of the position in which we should have found ourselves without them.

III. The Materials on which the Inscriptions have been recorded

The material on which the inscriptions have been recorded.

We have explained and illustrated the value of the Indian inscriptions. We come now to the consideration of the nature of them, from two points of view; as regards the materials on which they have been recorded, and as regards the topics of them.

It will be convenient to take first the materials on which the inscriptions have been recorded. These divide themselves into two leading categories; of metals, and of other substances than metal.

[1] With the initial date of Chandragupta in 320 B.C., Aśōka reigned from 264 to 227 B.C. (see JRAS, 1906. 984 ff.). He then (see ibid., 1904. 355) abdicated, and passed into religious retirement, as a Buddhist monk, in a cell on the mountain Suvarṇagiri, Sōngīr, one of the hills surrounding the ancient city Girivraja in Magadha, Bihār.

[2] AR, 4. Anniversary Discourse, 13, reprint of 1798.

A. Metals

1. Iron

Amongst the incriptions on metal, there is one that stands out by itself, in respect of the peculiarity of having been incised on iron. It is the short poem, constituting the epitaph of the Gupta king Chandragupta II. (F.GI, 139), which was composed in or about A.D. 415, and was placed on record on the iron column, measuring 23 ft. 8 inches in height, and estimated to weigh more than six tons, which stands at Meharaulī near Delhi. **Metals. Iron.**

The iron pillar itself is not unique. There is another, in fragments, which was apparently nearly twice the height of the Meharaulī column, at Dhār in Central India. But, while the Dhār column bears a Persian inscription of Akbar, incised in A.D. 1591–92, and a few names and letters in Nāgarī as well as Persian characters, there is no original record on it, placed there when it was set up.

2. Gold and Silver

On gold, we have a short Buddhist votive inscription from one of the Stūpas or relic-mounds at Gangu near Sir-Sukh in the Punjab[1] (ASI, 2. 130). **Gold and silver.**

On silver, we have a short record, not yet deciphered, from the Stūpa at Bhaṭṭiprōlu in the Kistna District of Madras (ASSI, 6. 13); and another, apparently dedicatory, on a small disc which was found in a Stūpa at Māṇikiāla in the Rāwalpiṇḍī District of the Punjab (ASI. 2. 160).

3. Brass

Records on brass are more numerous. Amongst them we may mention prominently the following:— **Brass.**

From a Stūpa at Wardak in Afghānistān, we have a brass relic-vase with an inscription the date of which falls in 6 B.C. (*Ariana Antiqua*, 118; JRAS, 1863. 255).

From Kōsam near Allahābād, we have an inscribed brass seal-ring, apparently of the Gupta period (ASI, 10. plate 2, No. 4).

From somewhere near Gayā, we have a brass image of Buddha, bearing on its pedestal an inscription which, marking

[1] It must be explained that 'Punjab' is the prescribed official form of the name which, otherwise, it is customary to present as 'Panjāb.' There may perhaps be noticed in this chapter a few other place-names, in respect of which comments might be made.

the image as a votive gift, is also of special interest in presenting a specimen of the nail-headed alphabet (IA, 19. 77).

And from the Chambā State there have been obtained some brass images, bearing inscriptions which give the names both of the king who caused them to be made and of the workmen who made them[1].

4. Bronze

Bronze. On bronze, we have some interesting stamps for making seals (JRAS, 1901. 98, plate, Nos. 8, 9, 11, 12, 14; 1905. 814, plate, Nos. 17 to 20); and one of them (No. 20) is of particular interest in presenting its legend in three classes of characters, Brāhmī, Kharōshṭhī or Kharōshṭrī[2], and Greek.

We also have a bronze head, obtained at Peshāwar, bearing round the base of it an inscription, which cannot be deciphered fully from the illustration of it, but seems to mark it as a votive offering (JASB, 5, 1836. 484, and plate 26).

The majority of the seals attached to the copperplate records mentioned farther on—at any rate, the more elaborate ones, of later date—must probably be held to be in reality of bronze: casting in copper would hardly have brought out the details of the devices and legends so completely.

And skilled examination would perhaps stamp as being of bronze, rather than copper, the signet-ring of the Mahārāja Mahēśvaranāga which is noticed on page 31 below.

5. Copper

Copper. For the most part, however, the known inscriptions on metal were placed on sheets of copper, ranging in size from about 2½ inches by 1⅞ inches in the case of a small and very early record obtained at Sōhgaurā in the Gōrakhpūr District, United Provinces of Agra and Oudh (JRAS, 1907. 509), to as much as about 2 ft. 6 inches square in the case of a record of 46 B.C. obtained at Suē-Vihār in the neighbourhood of Bahāwalpur in the Punjab (IA, 10. 324; 11. 128).

Some of these records on copper were commemorative and dedicatory, and were deposited inside the erections—relic-mounds, and, in the case of the Suē-Vihār plate, a tower—to which they belonged.

[1] *Annual Report of the Archaeological Survey of India* for 1902-3. 242; see also ASI, 14. plate 28.

[2] It is usual to follow Professor Bühler in using the form 'Kharōshṭhī.' But it is by no means certain that M. Sylvain Lévi is not right in holding that the real name of these characters is 'Kharōshṭrī.'

The usual copper record, however, was a donative charter, in fact a title-deed, and passed, as soon as it was issued, into private personal custody. And many of the known records of this class have come to notice through being produced by the modern possessors of them before official authorities, in the expectation of establishing privileges which (it is hardly necessary to say) have long since ceased to exist through the lapse of time, the dying out of families of original holders, rights of conquest, and the many changes of government that have taken place. It is, therefore, in private hands that we must still look to find the majority of those that remain extant but unknown. But others have been found buried in fields, and hidden in the walls and foundations of buildings. And the decay of old erections, and the excavation of ancient sites, may at any time yield a rich harvest in this direction.

A point that must always be borne in mind in connexion with these donative records on copper is that many of them have, in the course of time, passed from hand to hand and place to place, so as to have been discovered, like coins, inscribed gems, seals, seal-stamps, images, and other portable articles, in localities far distant from those to which they really belong. We have a pointed instance of this in the so-called Vakkalēri plates (EI, 5. 200). They contain a charter issued by the Western Chalukya king Kīrtivarman II. in A.D. 757. The grant was made when the king was encamped at a place specified in the record itself as Bhaṇḍāragaviṭṭage, on the north bank of the river Bhīmarathī; that is (see EI, 6. additions and corrections, A), at the modern Bhaṇḍār-Kauṭhēṁ, on the north bank of the Bhīmā, about twenty miles south-west from Shōlāpūr in the Bombay Presidency. And probably the plates were prepared and issued at that place, and were sent thence to the donee by a special officer, frequently mentioned in other similar records as the Dūtaka, 'the messenger.' But, whatever may have been the case in that respect, the charter conveyed a village named Suḷḷiyūr, situated in the immediate vicinity of Hāngal in the Dhārwār District. And the grantee must have resided somewhere there, on or close to the property that was given to him; and he must have had the record there in his possession, for production in case his title to the property should ever be questioned. The plates, however, eventually found their way to, and came to light from, the village of Vakkalēri in a distant part of Mysore.

The result of this peculiarity is as follows. A stone record almost invariably establishes the sovereignty or other jurisdiction, at the place itself where it stands, of any king, etc., by whose orders or in whose time it was drawn up. But, in the case of a copper charter, any such question usually depends entirely upon a successful identification of any places mentioned in it; and the find-places of such records frequently do not help us at all in this matter, except in indicating localities in which we may look first in the process of identification. To emphasize the point, and to prevent constantly occurring misconceptions, we shall have, some day, to rename all the copper records more precisely. The so-called Vakkalēri plates would be more correctly described as the Suḷḷiyūr grant: as regards its historical bearing, it is the country round Hāngal in the Dhārwār District, Bombay, not the Kōlār District in Mysore, which this record places in the territory of Kīrtivarman II. Another pointed case is that of the seal of the Maukhari king Śarvavarman (F.GI, 219), which was found at Asīrgaṛh in the Nimāṛ District, Central Provinces, some fifty miles to the south of the Narbadā: it is unmistakably a record of Northern India; and it had no original connexion with the locality in which it was found.

It may be added that, in view of the nature of the purport of nearly all the records on copper, epigraphists are in the habit of speaking of them as 'grants,' using the term 'inscriptions' more particularly in connexion with the records on stone. But, as will be made clear in the next section, there is no radical difference in nature, such as might be inferred from this difference in nomenclature, between the records of the two classes. The inscriptions on stone are for the most part donative charters, just as is the case with the large majority of the inscriptions on metal. On the other hand, some of the copper records are, like some of the stone records, simply commemorative or dedicatory.

The copper records call themselves sometimes *paṭṭikā*, 'a tablet, a plate' (e.g., EI. 1. 7, line 51), and sometimes *tāmra-paṭṭikā*, 'a copper tablet' (e.g., IA, 5. 52, line 34). But the expression more usually met with is either *śāsana*, 'a charter' (e.g., F.GI, 240, line 61), or *tāmra-śāsana*, 'a copper charter' (e.g., F.GI, 108, line 10). The term *triphalī-tāmra-śāsana*, 'a triplicate copper charter,' is found (EI, 3. 345) in the case of three separate records which are copies of each other, except only in respect of the specification of the different villages conveyed by them. And two instances are known (IA, 13. 121, line 21; H.SII, 1. 151, line 89) of the use of the term *praśasti*, 'a eulogy,' which is elsewhere found only in connexion with records on stone.

The plates on which these inscriptions were incised vary greatly in the number of the leaves, in the size and shape of them, and in the arrangement of the records on them; partly, of course, according to the lengths of individual records, but also according to particular customs and fashions prevalent in different parts of the country and in different periods time. In some cases a single plate was used; and it was inscribed sometimes on only one side of it, sometimes on both. More often, however, more plates than one were used; and the number ranges up to as many as eleven in the case of the Kaśākūḍi record of the Pallava king Pallavamalla-Nandivarman, of some time about A.D. 733 to 747 (H.SII, 2. 342). When more plates than two were used, they were sometimes numbered (e.g., IA, 5. 50, 154, 176; 7. 191; EI, 1. 2; 5. 106; 6. 84, 315; 8. 143, 159). In a few records on stone, the lines were numbered (e.g., PSOCI, Nos. 116, 124, 141, 192); but no instance can be cited of that having been done in the case of a record on metal.

In the case of records on copper covering more plates than one, it was customary to string the plates together by one or two copper rings, passing through round holes in them; much after the fashion in which the leaves of Indian manuscripts are strung together by threads.

6. Seals of Copperplate Records

Seals of copper-plate records.

It was also customary that such of the records on copper as were donative charters should be authenticated. And the most usual method of giving the authentication was by attaching a copper or bronze reproduction of the royal seal.

This emblem of sovereignty and power, whether in the shape of an actual seal made from a stamp, or in the shape of a stamp or a signet-ring for making a seal, no doubt played in India quite as important a part, in many ways, as it has always played in other eastern lands and in the west. And, in support of our belief, we may appropriately quote the following instances. In one direction, in the line of romance, a dexterous use of the royal signet was made by Kālidāsa, in his well-known play, the plot of which hinges upon the recognition of his wife Śakuntalā by king Dushyanta being evoked by the sight of the ring which he had given her, incised with the letters of his name. So also, the signet-ring of the fugitive minister, with his name engraved upon it, plays a part in the Mudrārākshasa. In another direction, in the line of practical affairs, we learn from the *Life* of the Chinese pilgrim Hiuen-tsiang (Julien, 260; Beal, 190) that, when he finally took leave of king Harshavardhana of Ṭhāṇēsar and Kanauj, the king furnished him with letters, written on fine white cotton stuff and certified by impressions of his seal made in red wax, which the officers of his escort were to present in all the countries through which they conducted the Master, to the end that the princes of those countries should provide carriages or other means of conveyance for the Master even to the borders of China.

And to the seal of Harshavardhana there is another allusion, in the Harshacharita of Bāṇa, which is worth citing, not only because it is a happy one, but also because it is instructive in mentioning another manner in which it was customary to make the seal; namely, by stamping it on a ball or disc of clay. The Hebrews seem to have made seals in the same way: 'it is turned as clay to the seal,' or 'it is changed as clay under the seal' (Job xxxviii. 14). And the backs and other parts of some extant specimens of Indian clay seals show distinctly the lines and the graining of the palms of the hands in which the clay was held in making the impressions [1].

The passage in question in the Harshacharita (Kashmīr edition, 430; and see the translation by Cowell and Thomas, 198) sets out that, when king Harshavardhana was about to make his expedition against the king of Gauḍa, a starting-point was selected, and a temporary encampment was made, at a suitable place, not far from his capital, on the bank of the river Sarasvatī. There the Grāmākshapaṭalika, or keeper of the village-records, came before the king, and asked him to issue the orders for the day, and presented a newly made golden stamp (*mudrā*), bearing the device of a bull, wherewith he was to make a seal authenticating the orders. As soon, however, as a ball or disc of clay was produced for that purpose, the stamp slipped from the king's hand, and fell face downwards upon some almost dry black mire which served as an inking-pad, and then rolled onto a spot of soft clay. And so the lines of letters of the legend on the stamp were distinctly marked on the bank of the river. The bystanders saw in that a bad omen. But the king deduced from it the auspicious augury, that the whole earth should be stamped with the single seal of his sole command.

[1] See JRAS, 1901. 103; also *Annual Report of the Archaeological Survey of India* for 1903-4. 101.

Here, plainly, Harshavardhana was to have used, not a signet-ring, but a stamp of the same kind with some which have been mentioned on page 26 above, under the heading of inscriptions on bronze.

Indian kings, princes, and high ministers, however, used also signet-rings, with which they could make their seals as occasion might require, or, of course, which they might themselves exhibit when necessary, or might entrust to others to be used as a voucher or token. Not only do we gather that from the Abhijñānaśakuntala and the Mudrārākshasa, but also we have an actual specimen of such a ring, referable to the fourth century A.D., which was obtained at Lahore (F.GI, 282). That specimen is an exaggerated signet-ring, made of copper or bronze, closely resembling the ordinary English pattern, and of the kind which may still be seen worn loosely on the thumbs of ministers of Native States. From the flat surface of the signet to the bottom of the ring, it is about $1\frac{1}{4}$ inches high. The surface of the signet is about $\frac{1}{16}$ inch thick, and is slightly oval in shape, about $1\frac{7}{8}$ by $1\frac{5}{8}$ inches. On it there is a legend, in two lines, of which the purport is: 'The Mahārāja Mahēśvaranāga, son of Nāgabhaṭṭa;' above the legend, and separated from it by a line serving the same purpose with the bar which usually stands below the heraldic device on an English signet-ring, there is a bull couchant, with a crescent moon; and below the legend there is a snake. The legend is in reverse in the original; and both it and the devices are sunk in the surface of the signet. Accordingly, if pressed, uninked, on some soft substance, this signet-ring would bring out the legend and devices in relief on a plain flat ground. If inked and then pressed on such a substance, it would bring them out in white relief on a black ground; as, we are to understand, was done by Harshavardhana's stamp according to Bāṇa. If inked and pressed on some hard substance, or on cloth stretched tight[1], it would bring them out in white on a black field.

This custom of thus attaching the royal authentication to charters has given us a large and highly interesting series of ancient Indian seals, some of them presenting devices only, others only legends, and others both legends and devices, and some of them being of an extremely elaborate kind. And

[1] For mention of the stamping of cloth fabrics, by way of ornamentation, but apparently not exactly in this fashion, see the Rājataraṁgiṇī, I. 294 f., 299.

from various statements in the records we know that the sole or the principal device, as the case may be, was almost always the *lāñchhana* or crest, which was usually different from the device emblazoned on the *dhvaja* or banner (see F.DKD, 299, note 4). The same device, the crest, was used on coins also, and sometimes with inscriptions on stone. And it usually took the form of some animal; a bull, a boar, a lion, a tiger, a fish, the bird-man Garuḍa, the monkey-god Hanumat, and so on. It was probably largely used on shields also, though at present there can be cited to that effect only one indication, which is found in an inscription on stone at Baḷagāmi in Mysore (PSOCI, No. 205); in the sculptures, showing a battle-scene, in the bottom compartment of that stone, the shields on the right side distinctly bear animals, which are apparently in one case a lion and in the other a boar.

In the case of records on single plates, it was customary to weld or otherwise fasten the seals on to the plates themselves; sometimes at the left side, before the lines of the inscription (e.g., F.GI, 256; IA, 15. 112, 140; EI, 6. 133, 140), and sometimes at the top (e.g., JASB, 47, 1878. 384; 63, 1894. 58). For some instances of seals which were once attached in this way, but have become separated from the plates to which they belonged, reference may be made to the fine Bhitarī seal of Kumāragupta II. (JASB, 58, 1889. 85), and to the still more elaborate Aśīrgaṛh seal of the Maukhari king Śarvavarman (F.GI, 220). We have also a seal of Harshavardhana, from Sōnpat (F.GI, 230); but it is not in the same excellent state of preservation.

In the case of charters consisting of more plates than one, the seal was treated in another manner, and was made to serve as a safeguard in addition to being a mark of authentication. This was effected by attaching it to the single ring when there was only one, and to one of the two rings when there were two. And the usual process seems to have been, first to rivet or otherwise join the ends of the ring, and then to cast the seal over the joint, so that the component parts of the record could not be separated without intentionally severing the rings. The result is that most of the seals attached to the charters in this way imitate the shape of exaggerated signet-rings, of varying sizes. But, together with the seals fixed on to the plates themselves, they represent real seals, not reversed stamps for making seals. As has been mentioned on page 26 above, probably they are for the most part of bronze, rather than of copper.

In this class of seals, for some which bear devices only, reference may be made to the plates at IA, 5. 50; 6. 23; 7. 39, 161, 252; 8. 27, 44; 9. 35, 103, 124; 11. 112, 126, 161; 12. 160; EI, 2. 352; 3. 104, 276; 4. 244; JBBRAS, 15. 386; B.ESIP, 106. For some seals with legends only, see the plates at F.GI, 108, 234; EI, 3. 261; 4. 244. And, for some seals with both legends and devices, see the plates at F.GI, 128, 169, 194, 198, 296; IA, 1. 16; 6. 25, 33; 7. 17, 190, 253; 8. 47, 320; 12. 93, 267; 13. 137, 249; 18. 234; 19. 310; EI, 2. 364; 3. 104; 4. 244; 6. 294; JRAS, 1865. 247; JASB. 86, 1897. 124; B.ESIP, 106. Some of the references given above illustrate clearly also the various shapes of rings and diverse methods of attaching the seals to them.

Sometimes an additional authentication was given by what purported to be more or less an autograph signature of the king or prince from whom a charter emanated, usually introduced by words meaning either 'this is the own hand of me' or 'this is the pleasure of me.' The signature is sometimes in characters of the same class with those used in the body of the record (e.g., IA, 6. 19, 193; 16. 202, 206; EI, 1. 317; 4. 210; 6. 294), and sometimes in different characters (e.g., IA, 13. 79; 14. 210; PSOCI, No. 282). Occasionally it is accompanied by marks evidently intended to represent some kind of a sign-manual (e.g., IA, 6. 19; 14. 201; EI, 6. 294).

There are a few cases in which an image was employed instead of a seal. The ends of the ring on which were strung the Khārēpāṭaṇ plates, bearing the record of the Śilāhāra prince Raṭṭarāja of A.D. 1008, were welded into the base of a small image of Garuḍa (EI, 3. 301). In the case of the Paiṭhaṇ record of A.D. 1272 of the Dēvagiri-Yādava king Rāmachandra (IA, 14. 314), on a plain ring which holds the plates together there slides another ring which is let into the back of an image of Garuḍa about 8½ inches high. In the case of the Kamauli plates of king Vaidyadēva of Prāgjyōtisha, an image of Gaṇapati is ensconced in a spoon-shaped receptacle which secured the ring on which the plates were strung (EI, 2. 352).

The Paiṭhaṇ record of A.D. 1272, mentioned in the preceding paragraph, is an epigraphic curiosity in respect of its weight. It is on three plates, each measuring about 1 ft. 3 inches in width by 1 ft. 8½ inches in height, which are so massive as to weigh 59 lb. 2 oz.; and the weight of the ring on which they were strung, and of the image of Garuḍa which was secured to it by the other ring, is 11 lb. 12 oz. Thus, the total weight of this title-deed, which conveyed a village to fifty-seven Brāhmaṇs, is no less than 70 lb. 14 oz.; appreciably more than half a hundredweight.

B. Other Substances than Metal

Other substances than metal.

The inscriptions on other substances than metal are found on crystal; on clay, sometimes left to harden naturally, sometimes apparently hardened by some artificial means, and sometimes baked into terra-cotta or burnt into brick; on earthenware; and on stone in various forms. Inscribed wooden tablets and strips of leather secured by clay seals have been obtained in Central Asia; but it is not known that any such have been as yet found in India.

For the most part, whatever happened to be the material used, the records of this class were executed by engraving.

We have, however, a few written with ink on earthenware; from Bhōjpur, Sāñchi, and Andhēr in Central India (pages 40, 44, 45, below); from Chārsada in the North-West Frontier Province (page 40); and from Hidda in Afghānistān (*Ariana Antiqua*, 111, and 262, plate). Of these, the instances from Central India are the earliest, and are probably to be referred to the second or third century B.C.

And from the Ginja hill, in either the Allahābād District or the Rewah State, we have an inscription recorded by paint on a rock (ASI, 21. 119, and plate 30; EI, 3. 306, plate): it mentions a Mahārāja named Bhīmasēna; and it presents a date which places it either in A.D. 371 or in 5 B.C.[1] Other painted inscriptions, executed in that manner as an accompaniment to frescoes, have been found in the Buddhist caves at Ajaṇṭā in the Nizam's Dominions (ASWI, 4. 136, and plate 59).

In the case of votive tablets made of clay, the custom was to use incised stamps, prepared of course in reverse; with the result that, on the tablets on which the stamps were impressed, the inscriptions, as well as any devices accompanying them, stand out in relief. And the results are the same in the case of clay seals, made from reversed metal dies or from anything in the shape of a stone matrix.

The inscriptions on brick were either incised with a stilus, or stamped with a die, before the clay was burnt into brick.

[1] This may seem rather a wide range of doubt. The fact is that we require a better reproduction of the record, to enable us to appreciate it properly and arrive at any decisive opinion as to its period.

In the case of inscriptions on stone, the devices and symbols, dynastic, religious, and of other kinds, which accompany some of them in Northern India and a large number of them in Southern India, were in the earliest instances incised in outline; but they were nearly always sculptured in relief from the time, the seventh century, when the use of them began to be frequent, and the nature of them became more or less elaborate. The records themselves, however, of the period covered by this account, were but rarely treated so. The Musalmān inscriptions were, it is believed, nearly always carved in relief. And various Hindū inscriptions were done in the same way in the Musalmān period. But only one instance of a record prepared in that way, otherwise than on metal, can as yet be cited for the earlier period; it is an inscription on the pedestal of an image of Buddha, of the Gupta period, found in excavations recently made at Sārnāth[1].

We have noted, on page 28 above, certain names by which some of the copperplate records designate themselves. Amongst the records on stone, some of the edicts of Aśōka style themselves *dhamma-lipi*, 'a writing of religion.' Various other records mention themselves by such names as *śilā-śāsana*, 'a stone charter;' *śilā-lēkha*, 'a stone writing;' and *praśasti*, 'a eulogy.' And other terms which occur are *śāsana*, 'a charter' (EI, 3. 5, line 19); *kallu-śāsana*, 'a stone charter' (EC, 3. Nj, 139, line 29); and *vīra-śāsana*, 'a charter or record of heroism' (PSOCI, No. 191; EC, 7. Sk, 144, last line).

We have also, on page 27 above, mentioned, and indicated the necessity of bearing in mind, the liability to travel, which has led to some of the copper charters being found in localities far distant from those to which they really belong. Records on stone were necessarily not so much liable to leave their original sites. But it is known (see ASI, 1. 161; 5. 143; 14. 78; JRAS, 1906. 407) that the two columns, bearing edicts of Aśōka, which now stand at Delhi, were brought there in the latter half of the fourteenth century under the orders of Fīrōz Shāh Tughlak; one from Meerut, and the other from Baṛā Topra, in the Ambālā District, some fifty miles from the Siwālik Hills. And it is supposed that the similar column which stands at Allahābād was originally set up at Kauśāmbī; because it bears, in addition to other records, an order of Aśōka addressed to the officials of Kauśāmbī. Also, it may be added, the opinion has been expressed that the inscribed iron pillar

[1] See *Progress Report of the Archaeological Survey*, Northern Circle, 1905–6. 33.

which stands at Meharaulī, near Delhi (see page 25 above) may have been taken to that place from Muttra.

1. Crystal

Crystal. Only one record on crystal, which may be classed as an inscription, can be cited; evidently, the material was found too hard for any general use to be made of it in the inscriptional line. The record in question is scratched, rather than engraved, on the six faces, each about $\frac{3}{8}$ inch in breadth, of an hexagonal piece of crystal, measuring about $2\frac{1}{4}$ inches in breadth, and probably, as it is pierced by a hole through its axis, originally used for suspending round the neck as an amulet, which was found in the remains of a Buddhist Stūpa or relic-mound at Bhaṭṭiprōlu in the Kistna District of Madras (EI, 2. 324, plate; ASSI, 6. 11, and plates 1, 4, 5). The purport of the inscription (EI, 2. 329) is not at all certain; it may perhaps register a votive offering, made by a woman from a town named Nadapura, Nandapura, in recognition of recovery from a serious illness.

Along with many other articles, two crystal phials and one crystal casket were found in the Bhaṭṭiprōlu deposit; but there are no inscriptions on them, or on crystal articles found in similar deposits elsewhere. In connexion, however, with some of those articles, other expedients were adopted, to mark the nature of them, or to record the dedication of them.

A crystal relic-casket was found in the Stūpa No. 2 at Sōnārī, in the neighbourhood of the well-known Sāñchi in the Bhōpāl State, Central India. The casket itself was not inscribed. But inside it there was deposited a piece of stone, about $\frac{3}{4}$ inch long by $\frac{1}{2}$ inch broad, bearing an inscription on the front and back (C.BT, 121, 316, and plate 24, 'box' No. 1). The purport of the inscription (JRAS, 1905. 687) is: '(*Relics*) of the sainted (literally, the good man) Gotiputa-Dudubhisara (or Duṁdubhisara), of the Himavat region, an heir of the faith.' This record gives us an historic name, of one of the four companions of Kotīputta-Kassapagotta, the missionary who (see page 44 below) was sent to the Himālayas by Moggaliputta-Tissa, in the time of Aśōka; and it helps to furnish valuable corroboration of the account of that mission given in the Dīpavaṁsa, 8. 10.

A crystal casket, obtained from the remains of a Stūpa at Kōlhāpūr in the Bombay Presidency, was found inside a stone box. Here, again, the crystal casket was not inscribed; but on the lid of the stone box there was engraved an inscription

(ASWI, No. 10, Cave-Temple Inscriptions, 39, and plate No. 1) to the purport: 'The gift of Bamha; caused to be made by Dhamaguta.'

2. Clay, Terra-cotta, and Brick

In various parts of India there are found, in large numbers, small inscribed tablets of clay, sometimes baked into terra-cotta, sometimes left to harden naturally. These tablets are called, as a matter of convenience, sometimes seals, sometimes discs; but neither term is exactly appropriate. The latter because these tablets are not uniformly round in shape: some of them are oval; others, rectangular. The former, because, for the most part, the nature of them is not such as to answer to any ordinary meaning of the word seal: they were mostly votive offerings. **Clay, terra-cotta, and brick.**

The best-known instances of these tablets are Buddhist, and bear the verse, the so-called formula or creed, which (see the Vinayapiṭaka, ed. Oldenberg, 1. 40) was pronounced by Assaji, one of the earliest followers of Buddha, and led to the conversion of those two persons, Sāriputta-Upatissa and Moggallāna-Kōlita, who became the chief disciples of Buddha. Sāriputta had asked Assaji who his teacher was, and what might be the essence of his doctrine. And Assaji replied: 'Of those conditions which spring from a cause, Tathāgata (Buddha) has declared the cause and the suppression of them; it is of such matters that he, the great Samaṇa, discourses.'

Of these votive tablets, some present the verse only (see, for instance, ASI, 11. plate 12, No. 13). Others exhibit with the verse a representation of a Stūpa (ibid., No. 12). Others exhibit, as an accompaniment, one or more Stūpas and perhaps a number of bells (ibid., plate 28, Nos. 2, 3). Others show, above the verse, and with an accompaniment of Stūpas, sometimes a Buddha seated on a throne, in the act of teaching (C.MG, plate 24, C), but more usually a Buddha squatting in the posture of meditation (ibid., D, E, F).

Others of these objects present, instead of the verse, other inscriptions, varying in length, some of which may be worth studying (C.MG, plate 24, Nos. 5, 6; ASI, 11. plate 28, No. 1); but the characters are so small that they are very difficult to read.

In short, the varieties of these Buddhist votive tablets are numerous; and it may be remarked here that in some cases the substance from which they were made was, not clay, but lac or wax (ASI, 3. 158, and plate 46, Nos. 2, 3). In some of the deposits, along with the usual Buddhist tablets there are found others, of the same make, but more of the nature of ordinary seals, which present sometimes devices only, sometimes only legends, and sometimes both legends and devices (ASI, 11. plate 12, Nos. 1 to 10). In one case we have, not a tablet prepared for presentation, but a stamp or mould, technically a matrix, for making such tablets (ASI, 16. plate 13, bottom).

Such are the usual Buddhist votive tablets. Others of a different class come from Sunet or Sunit in the Ludhiāna District, Punjab, mixed with similar tablets which are not Buddhist: these have been as yet only partially examined; but some good specimens have been figured in JRAS, 1901. 98, plate.

Of these Sunet seals, some bear simply the dedication: 'To Śaṁkara and Nārāyaṇa;' that is, to the gods Śiva and Vishṇu. Others, bearing that dedication on the reverse, present the name of the dedicator on the obverse; for instance: '(*An offering*) of the illustrious Vishṇudāsa' (loc. cit., No. 1). Others bear no dedication, but present simply the name of the offerer. These seem, from the devices on them, to be impressions from ordinary matrices of seals, made in order to be presented as votive offerings. And they are likely, therefore, to present names which may be historic. We have one (No. 3) which exhibits a horse, standing towards a sacrificial post, with the legend *parākrama*; this reminds us at once of the legend *aśvamēdha-parākrama*, 'he whose prowess, or whose title Parākrama, (*was established*) by performing the horse-sacrifice,' which stands on some of the coins of the Gupta king Samudragupta. Another (No. 7) exhibits a lion, seated, with a staff, resembling a combination of a spear and a trident, bound with ribbons, and the legend: 'Of the illustrious Sūryamitra.' A third (No. 10) exhibits a horse, prancing, and the legend: 'Of Dharmasēna.'

A large and highly interesting collection of clay seals, of the fourth and fifth centuries, has recently been found in the course of excavations made at Basāṛ, Basāṛh, in the Muzaffarpūr District, Bengal[1]: the total number of specimens is about 720, with somewhat more than 1,100 seal-impressions, exhibiting approximately 120 varieties. Here the bulk consists of seals of officials, guilds, corporations, etc.; of seals of private individuals; of seals of temples; and of seals with religious

[1] *Annual Report of the Archaeological Survey of India* for 1903-4. 101 ff., and plates 40 to 42.

legends on them. One, however, bears the legend: 'Of the illustrious Ghaṭōtkachagupta,' in which we can hardly avoid recognizing a mention of the father, called simply Ghaṭōtkacha in the inscriptions, of the Early Gupta king Chandragupta I. Three others bear legends which mention Dhruvasvāminī, called in the inscriptions Dhruvadēvī, wife of Chandragupta II, and give us Gōvindagupta as another son of that king. Others bear legends which mark them as having been issued at Vaiśālī. Others bear legends which include the territorial appellation Tīrabhukti, whence came the modern name Tirhūt. The legends on others present Tīra, evidently as the locality from which the territory derived its designation.

Quite recently, a smaller but highly interesting find of clay seals has been made near Kasiā in the Gōrakhpūr District. Amongst these we have some, referred to about A.D. 400 (JRAS, 1907. 365), which mention the Makuṭabandhana, the coronation-temple of the Mallas of Kusinārā at which (see ibid., 1906. 661) the corpse of Buddha was cremated, and others which speak of 'the community of friars, from the four quarters, at the Mahāparinirvāṇa,' i. e., at the scene of the Great Decease, which was at Kusinārā. And more lately still there has been found, at the same place, a seal-stamp, the legend on which mentions 'the community of friars at the Vishṇudvīpa (Veṭhadīpa) monastery.' These will be of considerable importance towards determining the identity of the remains in that neighbourhood.

A distinctly historical clay seal-stamp has come from Kāṭhiāwār, in the Bombay Presidency, but, of course, though it is a southern record, does not necessarily belong to that territory. The face of it is slightly oval, measuring about 2½ inches by 3 inches (IA, 12. 274); and it exhibits the sun and moon, and an inscription, incised in reverse in four lines, of which the purport is: '(*Seal*) of the prince and commander-in-chief Pushyēṇa, son of the illustrious prince Ahivarman, whose royal pedigree extends back unbroken to Jayaskandha.'

And we probably have another, but simpler, historical specimen, in a terra-cotta seal found at Bulandshahr, United Provinces, which presents (IA, 18. 289) the devices of a conch-shell and something which may be a nautilus or an ear shown in section, or a wing, or a conventional representation of a wheel, with the name Mattila, perhaps of a king who is mentioned as Matila in the Allahābād inscription of Samudragupta.

An inscribed terra-cotta image of Buddha, referred to the fifth century A.D., has been found near Kasiā, in the Gōrakhpūr District[1].

There are no indications that the use of brick for inscriptional purposes was ever at all general in India, as it was in some other eastern lands.

But at Bhitarī in the Ghāzīpūr District, United Provinces, there have been found numerous bricks, bearing the inscription 'the glorious Kumāragupta' (ASI, 1. 94, plate 30), with reference to either the first or the second Gupta king of that name, of the fifth century. And other inscribed bricks, of later date, have been found at Shōrkōt in the Jhang District, Punjab (ASI, 5. plate 30), stamped with apparently directions for the placing of them by the builders.

At Gōpālpūr in the Gōrakhpūr District, there have been found some brick tablets bearing Buddhist Sūtras (JASB, 65, 1896. proceedings, 99), one of which is a version in Sanskṛit of a short sermon preached by Buddha at Śrāvastī.

And a brick tablet, found in a field in the Jaunpūr District, United Provinces, bears an inscription (JASB, 19, 1850. 454), dated in A.D. 1217, which registers a mortgage of some lands as security for a loan.

3. Earthenware

Earthenware.

Inscribed earthenware relic-receptacles have been found at Bhōjpūr near the well-known Sāñchi in the Bhōpāl State, Central India (C.BT, 331, 333, and plate 26; 335, 336, and plate 27, Nos. 4, 5), and at Andhēr in the same neighbourhood (ibid., 346, and plate 29, No. 5). And the first of these (331) is of some interest, because the inscription, recorded on its lid, which was coated with whitewash, was written with ink. Only traces of the letters, however, remain; no part of the record is decipherable.

Three earthenware jars, bearing inscriptions in Kharōshṭhī characters written in ink, have been obtained at the Pālāṭu-Ḍherī hillock in the neighbourhood of Chārsada, North-West Frontier Province[2]: the inscriptions record the gift of the jars to the local community of Buddhist monks.

And from Kāṭhiāwār we have a piece of earthenware, apparently a fragment of a huge pot, bearing an incised inscription

[1] *Progress Report of the Archaeological Survey*, Punjab and United Provinces Circle, 1904–5. 51.

[2] *Annual Report of the Archaeological Survey of India* for 1902-3. 163; see also the *Report* for 1903–4. 289.

(IA, 14. 75) which presents a date equivalent to A.D. 566–67, and the name of 'the glorious Guhasēna,' who was one of the Maitraka princes of Valabhī.

4. Stone

We come now to the great bulk of the inscriptions, those which were recorded on stone in some form or another. They are found on rocks; on isolated monolith columns and pillars, of which some were erected simply to bear the records that were published on them, others were placed in front of temples as flagstaffs of the gods, and others were set up as pillars of victory in battle; on relic-receptacles, hidden away in the interiors of Buddhist Stūpas; on external structural parts of Stūpas; on façades, walls, and other parts of caves; on pedestals and other parts of images and statues, sometimes of colossal size; on moulds for making seals; on walls, beams, pillars, pilasters, and other parts of temples; and on specially prepared slabs and tablets, sometimes built into the walls of temples and other erections, sometimes set up inside temples or in the court-yards of them, or in conspicuous places in village-sites and fields, where they have occasionally in the course of time become buried. Stone.

(*a*) Rocks

Amongst the inscriptions on rocks, the most famous ones are those at Shāhbāzgarhī in the Yūsufzai country, at Mansehra in the Hazāra District, North-West Frontier Province, at Kālsī in the Dehra Dūn District of the United Provinces, at Girnār (Junāgaḍh) in Kāṭhiāwār, at Dhauli in the Cuttack District of Orissa, and at Jaugada in the Gañjām District of the Madras Presidency (see, for instance, C.IA, plates 1 to 7, 9 to 12; Senart, *Inscriptions de Piyadasi*, 1; and IA, 9. 282; 10. 83, 180, 209, 269; EI, 1. 16; 2. 447; ASSI, 1. 114), which present, more or less completely, and in different recensions, one series of the edicts of Aśōka (264 to 227 B.C.), the fourteen 'rock-edicts,' as distinguished from the 'pillar-edicts.' In these inscriptions of both series we have proclamations on the subject of religion and morality, issued by Aśōka for the guidance of his subjects, and placed on record in conspicuous positions in or near towns, or close to highways frequented by travellers and traders, or in the neighbourhood of sacred places visited by pilgrims. The idea of publishing some of them on rocks was certainly suggested by a reminiscence of the proclamations issued in the same way by the great Persian king Darius. And it can hardly be doubted that other traces Rocks.

of the influence of the Persian occupation of the valley of the Indus in the time of Darius are to be recognized in the style of address adopted both in the rock-edicts and in the pillar-edicts:—'Thus saith the king, the Beloved of the Gods, He of gracious mien,' and in the characters, Kharōshṭhī or Kharōshṭrī, in which the Shāhbāzgarhī and Mansehra versions were drawn up and incised.

The most notable inscribed rock is probably that at Girnār, which contains, in addition to the edicts of Aśōka, a record, with a date in A.D. 150, of the Mahākshatrapa Rudradāman (EI, 8. 36), and a record, with dates in A.D. 455 to 457–58, of the Gupta king Skandagupta (F.GI, 56).

Amongst other noteworthy inscriptions on rocks, we have the record of Aśōka at Sahasrām, Rūpnāth, and Bairāt in Northern India (C.IA, plate 14; IA, 6. 149; 7. 141; 20. 154), and at Brahmagiri, Śiddāpura, and Jaṭiṅga-Rāmēśvara in Mysore (JA, 1892, 1. 472; EI, 3. 134), which is dated (see JRAS, 1904. 26) 256 years after the death of Buddha in 482 B.C.[1], and (see ibid., 355) somewhat more than thirty-eight years after the anointment of Aśōka to the sovereignty in 264 B.C., and was framed when, having abdicated, he was living in religious retirement, as a fully admitted member of the Buddhist order, at Suvarṇagiri, Sōngīr, one of the hills surrounding the ancient city Girivraja, in Magadha. Others are the duplicate inscriptions in Brāhmī and Kharōshṭhī characters at Kanhiāra and Paṭhyār in the Kāngṛa District, Punjab (ASI, 5. 175; EI, 7. 116); the record of the Western Chalukya king Pulakēśin II. at Yekkeri in the Beḷgaum District, Bombay (EI. 5. 6); and various inscriptions on the Chandragiri hill in Mysore (EC, 2. Inscriptions at Śravaṇa-Beḷgoḷa, Nos. 1 to 35), including the epitaph of the Jain teacher Prabhāchandra (EI, 4. 22), which commemorates also the migration of the Digambaras to Southern India, and their settlement at Śravaṇa-Beḷgoḷa.

(*b*) **Columns and pillars**

Columns and pillars.

On columns we have the famous seven 'pillar-edicts' of Aśōka, at Allahābād (C.IA, plate 22; IA, 13. 306; EI, 2. 245),

[1] There are probably few writers, if any, who would now care to maintain 543 B.C. as the date of the death of Buddha: that is simply a Ceylonese invention of about the twelfth century A.D. Dates proposed more recently are 477, 508, and 487 B.C. For the determination by the present writer of 482 B.C. as the closest approximation to the truth that we are likely to attain, see JRAS, 1906. 984 ff.

at Delhi (C.IA, plates 18 to 21, Senart, *Inscriptions de Piyadasi*, 2; and IA, 17. 303; 18. 1, 73, 105, 300; IA, 13. 306; 19. 122; EI, 2. 245), and at Radhia, Mathia, and Rāmpūrwa in the Champāran District, Bengal (EI, 2. 245). And amongst the records of that king, published in this way, a very interesting one is the inscription on the column at Rummindēī, in the Nepalese Tarai (EI, 5. 4), which locates the Lumbinīvana garden in which Buddha was born.

The most notable inscribed column is probably that at Allahābād, which bears, in addition to Nos. 1 to 6 of the 'pillar-edicts,' two short Aśōka records which are known as the Queen's edict and the Kōsambī edict (C.IA, plate 22; IA, 19. 123, 124), and also the record of Samudragupta incised at some time about A.D. 375 (F.GI, 1).

A few other specially noteworthy inscriptions on columns and pillars are the following. At Ēraṇ in the Sāgar District, Central Provinces, we have the record of Budhagupta of A.D. 484 (F.GI, 88), invaluable because the full details of the date presented in it helped to enable us to determine the exact commencement of the Gupta era. At Mandasōr in Mālwā, we have on two battle-columns or columns of victory the record of Yaśōdharman (F.GI, 142, 149), who conquered the great foreign invader Mihirakula, and swept away the last remnant of the Gupta sovereignty. At Tāḷgund in Mysore, we have the record that recites the rise of the Kadamba dynasty of Western India (EI, 8. 24). From Mahākūṭa in the Bijāpur District, Bombay, we have the record, dated in A.D. 602, of the Western Chalukya king Maṅgalēśa[1] (IA, 19. 7; and see 32. 213). At Paṭṭadakal, in the same District, we have the duplicate record, in Nāgarī and Old-Kanarese characters, incised in A.D. 754, of the Western Chalukya king Kīrtivarman (EI, II. 3. 1). And at Śravaṇa-Beḷgoḷa, in Mysore, we have the epitaphs of the great Western Gaṅga prince Noḷambāntaka-Mārasiṁha, incised about A.D. 975 (EI, 5. 151), and of the Jain teacher Mallishēṇa, incised about A.D. 1129 (EI, 3. 184).

(*c*) Relic-receptacles

Amongst the inscriptions on relic-receptacles from the interiors of Buddhist Stūpas, we have most notably the record on the steatite or soapstone vase from Piprahwa (JRAS, 1906. 149; 1907. 105),—the oldest known Indian record, deposited perhaps within a century after the death of Relic-receptacles.

[1] The pillar bearing this record stands now in the compound of the Government Museum at Bijāpur.

Buddha,—which locates Kapilavastu, the paternal home of the great Teacher.

From the Stūpa No. 3 at the well-known Sāñchi in the Bhōpāl State, Central India, we have two steatite caskets which bear in ink, on the inner surfaces of the lids, in one case the letter *Sa*, and in the other case the letter *Ma* (C.BT, 299, and plate 22). They were found inside two boxes, apparently of ordinary stone, each bearing on its lid an incised inscription (C.BT, 297, and plate 22) to the following purport, explaining the initials: in one case: '(*Relics*) of Sāriputa;' in the other case: '(*Relics*) of Mahā-Mogalāna.' Here we have memorials of Sāriputta-Upatissa, and of Moggallāna-Kōlita, otherwise known as Mahā-Moggallāna, the two chief disciples of Buddha. Other relics of the same persons were deposited in inscribed steatite caskets in the Stūpa No. 2 at Satdhāra in the same neighbourhood (C.BT, 324, and plate 25, Nos. 4, 5).

From the Stūpa No. 2 at Sōnāri in the same neighbourhood, we have steatite vases bearing inscriptions (C.BT, 121, 317, and plate 24; and see JRAS, 1905. 681), of which the purport is as follows: in one case: '(*Relics*) of the sainted Kotīputa-Kāsapagota, the teacher of all the Himavat region;' and in another case: '(*Relics*) of the sainted Koḍiniputa-Majhima.' And from the Stūpa No. 2 at Sāñchi, we have an inscribed steatite casket containing relics of the same two persons, and of a third named Hāritīputa; and here, again, the record marks Kāsapagota as the teacher of all the Himavat region. The records are of extreme value in corroborating the account, given in the Buddhist books, of missions which were sent by the great priest Moggaliputta-Tissa, in the time of Aśōka, to establish the Buddhist faith in border-countries. And they are of particular interest in supporting, against the assertions of Buddhaghōsha in his Samantapāsādikā and of Mahānāma in the Mahāvaṁsa, the earlier statement of the Dīpavaṁsa, 8. 10, that the leader of the mission to the Himālayas was the Thēra Kassapagotta, and that Majjhima was only one of the companions sent with him.

Another steatite casket from the same deposit in the Sāñchi Stūpa No. 2 bears three inscriptions (C.BT, 289, and plate 20, No. 4), of one of which the purport is: '(*Relics*) of the sainted Mogaliputa.' Here, it can hardly be doubted, we have a memorial of the great Moggaliputta-Tissa himself, who has been mentioned just above. And we find another memorial of him in the inscription on a steatite vase from the Stūpa

No. 2 at Andhēr in the same neighbourhood (C.BT, 347, and plate 29, Nos. 8, 9), of which the purport is: '(*Relics*) of the sainted Mogaliputa, pupil of Gotiputa.' We have a memorial of Gotiputa on the same steatite casket from the Sāñchi Stūpa No. 2, mentioned just above, which bears the record of the relics of Moggaliputta.

From Andhēr we have, from the Stūpa No. 3, a steatite casket which bears two inscriptions (C.BT, 349, and plate 30, No. 6). One, incised on the outside, is to the purport: '(*Relics*) of the sainted Hāritīputa.' The other, of special interest because it was written in ink on the inside of the lid, is to the purport: 'The gift of Asadēva.'

The Bhaṭṭiprōlu Stūpa yielded also three inscribed stone relic-receptacles (ASSI, 6. plate 3), bearing nine short records (VOJ, 6. 148; EI, 2. 323). Two of the inscriptions mention a king whose name appears both as Kubiraka and as Khubiraka; and two of the others speak of relics of Buddha. A special interest attaches to these nine records, in that they exhibit some very exceptional palaeographic peculiarities, in a variety of the alphabet, referred to approximately the period 225 to 200 B.C., which is not met with elsewhere.

(*d*) External parts of Stūpas

Amongst the inscriptions recorded conspicuously on external parts of Stūpas, we may mention, in the first place, the record on a pillar of the eastern gateway of the Stūpa at Bharaut in the Nāgōd State, Central India (C.SB, plate 12; IA, 14. 138; 21. 227), which registers the fact that the *tōraṇa* or ornamental arched part of the gateway was caused to be made, and the completion of the masonry work was effected, by Vāchhiputa-Dhanabhūti, son of Gotiputa-Agaraju, son of the king Gāgīputa-Visadēva. This record is of special interest because it further refers itself to the time of the sovereignty of the Śuṅgas; it gives us the only known inscriptional record of that dynasty, which the Purāṇas place next after the great Maurya dynasty of Chandragupta and Aśōka.

External parts of Stūpas.

From the upper architrave of the southern gateway of the Sāñchi Stūpa No. 1, we have an inscription (C.BT, plate 19, No. 190) which mentions Siri-Sātakaṇi, one of the early kings of the Deccan and Central India.

From other external parts of the same Stūpa and the second one at the same place, we have a number of short records, registering gifts of various parts of the buildings (EI, 2. 87, 366), which, mentioning the places of abode of the donors, carry back to very early times various cities and towns which still exist, and still play their part in current events.

In the inscriptions on the pillars, rails, and copings of the Bharaut Stūpa (IA, 21. 225), we have a larger variety of records.

Some of them, donative records of the same nature with those at Sāñchi, are similarly useful in the geographical line. And three of them (loc. cit., Nos. 95, 134, 144) are of importance in showing that the Buddhist canon had already, in the second or first century B.C., divisions known by the names of the Pitaka, the Sūtrānta, and the Five Nikāyas.

Others, not of that class, but descriptive of the sculptures to which they are attached, are valuable in other directions. Some (C.SB, plates 25 to 27) carry back to the same period some of the Jātakas, the stories of the previous existences of Buddha in various forms. Three of them mention ancient kings (IA, 21. 227, Nos. 20, 58, 77): Janaka, with queen Sivaladēvī (C.SB, plate 44, top); Pasēnaji, of Kōsala (plate 13, right); and Ajātasatu, represented in the act of performing worship to Buddha (plate 16, right). One of them marks an illustration (C.SB, plate 13, left) of the *bōdhi*-tree of the last Buddha, Sakamuni; i.e., of the tree under which he was sitting when he attained perfect knowledge, enlightenment as to good and evil. Others mark sculptures (C.SB, plate 29, and 30, No. 1) of the *bōdhi*-trees of some of the previous Buddhas, whose names they present as Vesabhu, Konāgamena, Kasapa, Vipasin, and Kakusaḍha.

Amongst miscellaneous records, a notable inscription stamps a medallion (C.SB, plate 34, No. 2) as representing Mahadēva rescuing Vasuguta from the belly of a sea-monster; the scene shows Mahadēva seated with two companions in a boat over the sea-monster, an enormous fish, which is disgorging another boat containing Vasuguta and two attendants. Another stamps a panel (C.SB, plate 16, centre) as exhibiting the angel Arahaguta announcing to the great assembly the future conception of Buddha. Another marks a medallion (C.SB, plate 28, top, right) as showing the dream of Māyā, the mother of Buddha, in which she saw her future son about to enter into her womb in the form of a white elephant. Another marks a medallion (C.SB, plate 57) as illustrating the gift of the Jētavana park to the Buddhist community by Anādhapeḍika; the scene shows his servants putting down the layer of a crore of coins with which he purchased the site (see Vinayapiṭaka, 2. 159; Jātaka, 1. 92). Others record the names of statues of gods and goddesses, nymphs of heaven, celestial attendants, and other beings, and help much in the department of Buddhist mythology.

From the remains of a Stūpa at Muttra we have the lion-capital, covered with records, in intrusive Kharōshṭhī characters (JRAS, 1894. 525; 1904. 703; 1905. 154), which establish a temporary occupation of that part of India, just after the time of Huvishka, by a power from the north-west which was represented at Muttra by the governors Rajula-Rājuvūla and his son Śuḍasa-Śoḍāsa. And, from a rail outside the eastern gate of the Sāñchi Stūpa No. 1, we have an inscription (F.GI, 29) which gives us a date in A.D. 412 for the Gupta king Chandragupta II.

(*e*) Caves

Amongst the inscriptions on façades, walls, and other parts of caves, we have at the Bārābar and Nāgārjunī Hills in the Gayā District, Bengal (ASI, 1. 47, plate 20; C.IA, plate 16; IA, 20. 361), other records of Aśōka, and some of a king Daśaratha who according to the Vishṇu-Purāṇa was a grandson of Aśōka. Caves.

From the Hāthigumphā cave near Cuttack in Orissa, we have the record of king Khāravēla of Kaliṅga (see page 14 above), which belongs to 156–55 B.C. if it is really dated, as has been held, in the year 165 of the time of the Maurya kings.

From a cave at the Nānāghāṭ Pass in the Poona District, Bombay, we have the record of queen Nāyanikā, wife of one of the Sātavāhana-Sātakaṇi kings (PSOCI, No. 265; ASWI, 5. 6).

And from caves at Nāsik, Junnar, and Kārlē, we have the valuable records (ASWI, 4. 98 to 114; EI, 7. 56, 57, 61, 71; 8. 59 ff.) of the Kshaharāta king Nahapāna and his son-in-law Ushavadāta, and of Gōtamīputa-Sātakaṇi and his son Vāsiṭhīputa-Puḷumāyi, which throw so much light on the history of Western India in the first and second centuries A.D.

(*f*) Images and Statues

Amongst inscriptions on pedestals and other parts of statues and images, we may mention, as being either typical instances or otherwise of special interest, the record of a king or prince named Turāmala, dated in A.D. 7 or 8, on the base of a colossal statue of Buddha at Bōdh-Gayā (C.MG, plate 25); the record, dated in A.D. 22, on the base of a statue of the Jain Tīrthaṁkara Ara at Muttra (EI, 2. 321); the record, dated in A.D. 328, on the pedestal of a statue of Buddha at Hashtnagar in the Images and statues.

Peshāwar District (JASB, 58, 1889. 144; IA, 18. 257; 20. 394); the record of the time of Kumāragupta I, dated in A.D. 448, on the pedestal of an image of Buddha at Mankuwār in the Allahābād District (F.GI, 45); the record of the Mahārāja Bhīmavarman, dated in A.D. 458–59, on the base of a sculptured group of Śiva and Pārvatī at Kōsam near Allahābād (F.GI, 266); the record of the time of the foreign invader Tōramāṇa, the father of Mihirakula, on the colossal boar at Ēraṇ in the Sāgar District (F.GI, 158); the record of the Sthavira Mahānāma, on the pedestal of an image of Buddha at Bōdh-Gayā (F.GI, 278); and the record of the time of Ādityasēna, dated in A.D. 672, on the pedestal of an image of the sun at Shāhpūr in the Patna District (F.GI, 208).

There are some notable inscribed colossal statues of the Jain saint or god Bāhubalin or Bhujabalin, otherwise called Gummaṭa or Gommaṭēśvara, at Śravaṇa-Beḷgoḷa in Mysore, and at Kārkaḷa and Vēṇūr in the South Kanara District, Madras (EI, 7. 108 ff., and plates). But, while the statue at Śravaṇa-Beḷgoḷa dates from the period A.D. 977 to 984, the other two date only from A.D. 1432 and 1604 respectively.

Another noteworthy object in this class is the colossal statue found near Kasiā in the Gōrakhpūr District, United Provinces (ASI, 18. 57, and plate 5; 22. 17), which represents Buddha dying, and bears on a part of its pedestal an inscription (F.GI, 272) which is referable to about the end of the fifth century A.D.

(*g*) Moulds for making Seals

Moulds for making seals.

In the way of moulds or stamps for making seals, we must mention first some objects from Harappa in the Montgomery District, Punjab, of which two have been figured (ASI, 5. plate 33, No. 1; C.IA, plate 28; IA, 15. 1). They present legends in some characters the clue to the decipherment of which has not yet been obtained.

From a place which has come to be known as Sankīsā, or more fully Sankīsā-Basantpur, in the Farrukhābād District, United Provinces, we have a steatite or soapstone seal-stamp (ASI, 11. plate 9, No. 1), which presents the name Utarasēna, incised in reverse, with some emblem above it the nature of which is not apparent, and, below it, a *svastika* or square cross with four arms. And it may be added that from the same place we have a goldsmith's mould, also made of steatite (ibid., No. 6), bearing three Kharōshṭhī characters which seem to give a word in the genitive case: here the letters are not reversed, and they stand on the flat surface surrounding the hollow containing the pattern which was to be reproduced from the mould; they seem, therefore, to give the name of the owner of the mould.

In this line, however, the chief curiosity is the rock-cut seal-matrix, of about the commencement of the seventh century, at Rōhtāsgaṛh in the Shāhābād District, Bengal (F.GI, 283; and see C.MG, plate 27, G, for an illustration of the original as it actually stands, in reverse). This matrix exhibits a bull couchant, and below it a legend, of which the purport is: '(*Seal*) of the illustrious Mahāsāmanta Śaśāṅkadēva.' The device and the legend are surrounded by a circle, about 4¼ inches in diameter, marking the size of any impressions to be produced from it. And in the original the legend is in reverse, and, with the device, it is carved in the rock, not carved in relief. We plainly have here a matrix or mould for making seals. It is, however, difficult to imagine that so friable a substance as rock would stand having molten metal poured into it, and would remain unhurt. It would seem, either that some very soft metal must have been used, which could be forced into the mould in almost a cold state, or else that the mould was made for the purpose of producing a clay, lac, or wax seal.

Limitation of space precludes us from illustrating any more the various positions and circumstances in which the inscriptions on stone are found. And, for the same reason, we cannot enter here into a description of the sculptured devices, religious, dynastic, and of other kinds, which accompany a few of them in Northern India, and a large number of them in the South: these sculptures are of considerable interest in their own line; but they have not the particular importance which attaches to the seals of the copperplate records. We must pass on to our next division of the general subject.

IV. The Topics of the Inscriptions, and the Reasons for which they are Historically so Useful

The topics of the inscriptions, and the reasons for which they are historically so useful.

We have considered the inscriptions according to the substances on which they were recorded. We have now to examine the nature of them according to the purport of their contents; especially with the object of showing precisely why they are of such importance from the historical and chronological point of view.

A. Plain Statements of Events

Plain statements of events.

In classifying the inscriptions for this purpose[1], we may take first those of them which are plain statements of events, sometimes perhaps containing allusions to religion and to donations, but not specially directed to any such ends. In this class one of the best instances of purely historical narrative is the Hāthigumphā cave-inscription, already referred to (page 14 above), which summarizes the career of Khāravēla of Kaliṅga as far as the thirteenth year of his reign, and presents to us a chapter, or the beginning of a chapter, of a dynastic chronicle. Another is the eulogy of Samudragupta on the Aśōka column at Allahābād (F.GI, 1), which recites his pedigree, describes his conquests in Northern India, mentions some of the foreign tribes with which he had relations, and gives us a considerable insight into the political divisions of Southern India. A third is the short poem, in grand diction, given in duplicate on the two columns of victory at Mandasōr (F.GI, 142, 149), which describes the triumphs of Yaśōdharman, including the humbling of the great foreign invader Mihirakula 'who had never before that bowed his head in obeisance to any save the god Śiva.'[2]

To the same class we may refer some of the records of the carrying out of public works. Here we have the two fine rock-inscriptions at Junāgaḍh (EI, 8. 36 ; F.GI, 56), which record the repairing of the embankment of the great lake Sudarśana

[1] There are five epigraphs, of a quite exceptional nature, which cannot be placed in any of the following categories, and in fact hardly come under the heading of 'inscriptions' as defined on page 1 above, but which must not be left unnoticed.

From stones at Ajmēr we have fragments of two otherwise unknown plays. One of these plays, entitled Lalitavigraharājanāṭaka, was composed by a poet Sōmadēva in honour of the Chāhamāna king Vigraharāja. The other, entitled Harakēlināṭaka, was composed by Vigraharāja himself. These fragments have been edited by Professor Kielhorn in IA, 20. 201 ff., and in *Festschrift der Königlichen Gesellschaft der Wissenschaften zu Göttingen*, 1901.

From a stone at Dhār, in Central India, we have the first two acts of an otherwise unknown play by Madana, entitled Pārijātamañjarī or Vījayasrī, of which the hero is the Paramāra king Arjunavarman. These have been edited by Professor Hultzsch, in EI, 8. 96 ff., and separately.

And from other stones at Dhār we have two Prākṛit poems, odes to the tortoise incarnation of Vishṇu, written in honour of king Bhōja. These have been edited by Professor Pischel, in EI, 8. 241 ff.

[2] Something of the same kind—at any rate, a firm resolve to that effect from childhood upwards—is claimed in the Harshacharita for Bhāskaravarman, king of Prāgjyōtisha : see the translation by Cowell and Thomas, 217; Kashmīr text, 460.

in the time of Rudradāman, and again in the time of Skandagupta; the former of them reciting, also, how the lake was originally made by a governor of the great Maurya king Chandragupta, and had been embellished by a governor of Aśōka. And here we have also the Tāḷgund inscription (EI, 8. 24), which, directed primarily to recording the construction of a great tank, recites, by way of introduction, the origin and rise to power of the early Kadamba dynasty of Banawāsi.

To the same class belong some of the epitaphs: for instance, the charming short poem on the iron pillar at Meharaulī (F.GI, 139), which preserves the memory of the great Gupta king Chandragupta II; the panegyric of the great Western Gaṅga prince Noḷambāntaka-Mārasiṁha at Śravaṇa-Beḷgoḷa (EI, 5. 151); and the epitaphs of the Jain teachers Prabhāchandra and Mallishēṇa at the same place (EI, 4. 22; 3. 184).

In the same class we have some of the monumental pillars and tablets commemorating the death of heroes in battle. Here we may cite the small pillar at Ēraṇ (F.GI, 91), which gives us the name of king Bhānugupta, as a preliminary to recording how his follower Gōparāja died in fight, and how Gōparāja's wife accompanied his corpse onto the funeral pyre. And other instances are found in the *vīrgals* or 'hero-stones' of Central India, Bombay, and Madras, as illustrated by the Tērahi stones (IA, 17. 201), which recite how Chāṇḍiyana, the governor of a fortress under Guṇarāja, was killed in a fight between Guṇarāja and Undabhaṭa; by the Ablūr stone (EI, 5. 261), which commemorates the death of the brothers Mācha and Gōma, fighting valiantly on the occasion of a cattle-raid against their village; and by the Kīḻ-Muṭṭugūr, Āmbūr, Naregal, and Baṅgavādi tablets (EI, 4. 178, 182, 183; 6. 162; 7. 22), which preserve the memory of other heroes killed on occasions of the same kind.

In the way of more miscellaneous records referable to this same class, we have the Sōhgaurā plate (JRAS, 1907. 509), containing a public notification of the establishment of two storehouses, at the junction of three great highways of vehicular traffic, to meet any emergent needs of persons using those roads; the Mandār Hill rock-inscriptions (F.GI, 211), which record the construction of a tank by the order of Kōṇadēvī, the wife of king Ādityasēna; and the Bhumarā pillar (F.GI, 110), which was set up as a boundary-mark between the territories of the Mahārāja Hastin and the Mahārāja Śarvanātha, and the record on which enables us to synchronize the families to which those two princes belonged.

And here we may mention also another stone at Kīḷ-Muṭṭugūr (EI, 4. 179), which marks the spot on an embankment at which a local hero killed a tiger; the Kōṭūr inscription (IA, 20. 69), which narrates how a Śaiva ascetic immolated himself in the fire; and the Beḷatūru inscription (EI, 6. 213), which tells the pathetic tale of how, in spite of the remonstrances of her parents and her relatives, the wife of a local governor entered the flames, to accompany her dead husband to the world of the gods.

In the same class we may notice two inscriptions at Śīyamaṅgalam and Tiruvottūr[1], which give an interesting insight into the administration of criminal law in the twelfth century. One of them recites how a certain individual by mistake shot a man belonging to his own village; whereupon, the governor and the people of the district assembled together, and decided that the culprit should not die for the offence committed by him through inadvertence, but should burn a lamp in the Tūnāṇḍār temple at Śīyamaṅgalam; and accordingly he provided sixteen cows, from the milk of which ghee was to be prepared, to be used in burning the lamp. The other records that a man went hunting, and missed his aim, and shot another man; whereupon, the people of the district assembled, and decided that the culprit should make over sixteen cows to, apparently, the Tiruvottūr temple.

We may further include here two inscriptions at Cheṅgama[2], which embody political compacts of alliance for purposes of offence and defence. And, though it does not contain any narrative, we may conveniently note here the seal-matrix of Śaśāṇka, cut in the rock at the hill-fort of Rōhtāsgaṛh (see page 49 above),—a mould for casting seals to be issued by him,—which, by its existence there, locates in that direction the kingdom of Kie-lo-na-su-fa-la-na mentioned by the Chinese pilgrim Hiuen-tsiang.

B. Records due to Religious Motives

Records due to religious motives. For practically all such records as those mentioned in the preceding paragraphs, we are indebted to an historical instinct which found expression more or less fully in them. And some of them illustrate how well the ancient Hindūs could put together brief historical narratives, concise and to the point,

[1] See the *Annual Report of the Government Epigraphist*, 1899–1900. 11, para. 26.

[2] See ibid., 13, paras. 32, 33.

but limited in scope. But the records of that class, though fairly numerous in themselves, are but few in number in comparison with the others that we have yet to deal with. For the great bulk of the epigraphic materials that have come down to us, we are indebted, not to any historical instinct of the Hindūs, but to the religious side of their character, and to their desire for making endowments on every possible occasion.

In the class of inscriptions to which we have now come, we may take first those for which we are indebted to religious motives alone. And, amongst them, we may notice first those which were directed to the propagation of religion and morality. Here, however, we can bring forward prominently only some of the records of Aśōka.

We have, in the first place, his well-known rock and pillar edicts (see pages 41, 42, above), scattered about at various places of importance in his dominions and in other territories that were more or less subject to his influence, from Shāhbāzgarhī in the Yūsufzai subdivision of the Peshāwar District on the north to Śiddāpura in Mysore on the south, and from Dhauli in the Cuttack District and Jaugada in the Gañjām District on the east to Girnār (Junāgaḍh) in Kāṭhiāwār on the west. The object of them was to proclaim the firm determination of Aśōka to govern his realm righteously and kindly in accordance with the duty of pious kings, and with considerateness for even religious beliefs other than the Brāhmaṇical faith which he himself at first professed, and to acquaint his subjects with certain measures that he had taken to that end, and to explain to them how they might co-operate with him in his objects. But, in addition to mentioning the contemporaneous foreign kings Antiochus I. or II. of Syria, Ptolemy Philadelphus of Egypt, Antigonus Gonatas of Macedonia, and Magas of Cyrene, they yield items of internal history, in detailing some of Aśōka's administrative arrangements; in locating the capital of his empire at Pāṭaliputra (Patna), and seats of viceroys at Ujjēni (Ujjain) and Takhasilā (Taxiḷa); in giving the names of some of the leading peoples of India, particularly the Chōḷas, the Pāṇḍyas, and the Andhras; and in recording the memorable conquest of the Kaliṅga country, the attendant miseries of which first directed the thoughts of the king to religion and to solicitude for the welfare of all his subjects.

To these we must add that record of Aśōka, extant in various versions in Northern India and in Mysore (see page 42 above), which was framed and issued when he had been converted to Buddhism and had been led to formally join the Buddhist order, and when, having taken the vows of a monk, he had abdicated, and was spending his remaining days in religious retirement in a cave-dwelling on Suvarṇagiri (Sōngīr), one of the hills surrounding the ancient city of Girivraja in Magadha (Bihār). This record was issued to proclaim Buddhism as the true religion, and Buddha, 'the Wanderer,' the ascetic teacher exiled by his own choice from the house-life into the houseless state, as the great exponent of it. And it has its historical value in the fact that it was framed (see JRAS, 1904. 26, 355) when 256 years had elapsed after the death of Buddha, and 38 years after the anointment of Aśōka to the sovereignty, and, it may be added, on the first anniversary of his abdication. It thus confirms exactly, and carries back to the time of Aśōka himself, the statement of the Ceylonese chronicle, the Dīpavaṁsa, that 218 years intervened between the death of Buddha and the anointment of Aśōka. Corroborating the Dīpavaṁsa in that important matter, it enables us to accept with considerable confidence the historical details given for the intervening period by the same chronicle. And it enables us to determine (see JRAS, 1906. 984 ff.), with due regard to all the considerations that have to be harmonized, and to put forward as the closest approximations that we are likely to attain, 482 B.C. for the death of Buddha, alongside of 320 B.C. for the foundation of the Maurya sovereignty by Chandragupta, and 264 B.C. for the anointment of Aśōka.

To religious motives alone, in the form of the desire to honour the memory of saints and teachers by enshrining relics of them, we owe the records on relic-caskets of Kotīputta-Kassapagotta and Koḍinīputta-Majjhima and Gotīputta-Dundubhissara, from Sāñchi and Sōnārī (see JRAS, 1905. 681, 685, 687), which confirm in so important a manner the account given in the Dīpavaṁsa of the missions that were sent out by the great priest Moggaliputta-Tissa, in the time of Aśōka, to establish the Buddhist faith in the border-lands.

Similarly, to the desire to honour in another way the memory of a dead teacher we owe the Rummindēī pillar-inscription of Aśōka (EI, 5. 4), which is of such interest because it localizes the Lumbinīvana garden, the place of Buddha's birth. The record, framed when Aśōka was twenty-years-anointed, and before his conversion to Buddhism, tells us that he did the place the great honour of visiting it in person, evidently in the course of some tour of inspection or state-progress through the north-eastern parts of his dominions; and it proceeds to recite that, because Buddha, 'the Sakya saint,' was born there, the king built a stone enclosing and screening wall round the place, and set up a stone column (the one which bears the record), and made the village Lumminigāma free of certain taxes.

So, again, to the installation of relics of Buddha we are indebted for the inscriptions of about A.D. 15 on the Muttra lion-capital (JRAS, 1894. 525; 1904. 703; 1905. 154), which, amongst other items of information, mention the Satraps Rajula-Rājuvūla and Śuḍasa-Śoḍāsa; and for the record on the Sir-Sukh or Taxila plate (EI, 4. 54), which gives us a date in A.D. 22 for the Satrap Patika.

And to another development of the same desire we are indebted for the oldest known Indian record, the inscription on the Piprahwa relic-vase (see page 43 above), which was directed to preserving the memory of the kinsmen of Buddha, the Ṣakyas of tradition, who were ruthlessly massacred, men, women, and children, by Viḍūḍabha, king of Kōsala, and which locates for us the city Kapilavastu, the home of Buddha in his childhood, youth, and early manhood.

We owe the record (IA, 14. 138; 21. 227) which proves the historical existence of the dynasty of the Śuṅgas, to the building of a gateway of the Stūpa at Bharaut. And we owe the Kura inscription of Tōramāṇa (EI, 1. 238) to the erection of a Buddhist monastery.

We owe the Nānāghāṭ inscription, of the Sātavāhana-Sātakaṇi series (ASWI, 5. 60), to the desire to commemorate the great sacrifices that had been celebrated, and the costly sacrificial fees that had been given, by queen Nāyanikā.

For the inscription of Tōramāṇa on the breast of the stone boar at Ēraṇ (F.GI, 158), which establishes his conquest of Central India, we are indebted to the building of the temple, in the portico of which the boar stands. And to the same motive we are indebted for the Gwālior inscription of his son Mihirakula (F.GI, 161), and for the Aihoḷe inscription of Pulakēśin II. (EI, 6. 1), which contains a great deal of important historical and geographical matter, and for the Vaḷḷimalai inscription (EI, 4. 140), which settles the first four generations of the family of the Western Gaṅga princes of Taḷakāḍ.

It is to the restoration of a temple that we are indebted for the important Mandasōr inscription (F.GI, 79), which gave us what had so long been wanted, namely, a date for one of the Early Gupta kings, recorded in an era, capable of identification, other than that which was specially used by them in their own records. And we owe another important record of the Early Guptas, the Ēraṇ pillar-inscription (F.GI, 88), which gives us the name of Budhagupta and one of the dates which helped to fix the exact initial point of the Gupta era, to the erection of the column as the 'flagstaff' of the god of the temple in front of which it stands.

To the installation of an image of the Jain saint Vardhamāna, we owe the Muttra inscription (EI, 1. 381; IA, 1904. 34, No. 4), which gives us a date in the year 5, falling in 53 B.C., for Kanishka. To the installation of an image of a Bōdhisattva we owe another record from the same place (IA, 1904. 39, No. 9), which gives us a date in the year 33, in 24 B.C., for Huvishka; and for another record (JBBRAS, 20. 269), which gives us a date for the same king in the year 45, in 12 B.C., we are indebted to the installation of an image of Buddha. To the installation of another image of a Bōdhisattva we owe the record from the place known as Sēt-Mahēt (EI, 8. 180), which seems to give conclusive evidence as to the position of the ancient city Śrāvastī. And we owe the Shāhpur inscription (F.GI, 208), which gives us a date for king Ādityasēna, recorded in the Harsha era and falling in A.D. 672–73, to the installation of an image of the Sun.

The Takht-i-Bahaī inscription of Gondophernēs, of A.D. 47 (see page 5 above), so interesting in view of the corroboration which it gives to the Christian tradition of the mission of St. Thomas the Apostle to the east, was recorded to register some pious act performed, in memory of his parents, by the person for whom the record was drawn up.

To the building of a temple of the Sun, under the name Chaṇḍasvāmin, we are indebted for the Dhōlpūr inscription of A.D. 842 (ZDMG, 40, 1886. 39), which, in specifying its date in the era of 58 B.C. as the year 898 of 'the time called *vikrama*,' in the sense of a reckoning of years commencing in the autumn, which was the 'war-time,' the season for undertaking campaigns, gives us the earliest known instance of the use of the precise term from which there was evolved the legend (see page 4 above, and note 2) that the era was founded by a king named Vikrama.

A dispute between two priests, each of whom claimed the ownership of a particular plot of land for his god, has given us an interesting record of a trial by ordeal in an inscription at Kittūr (JBBRAS, 9. 307).

The settlement of a sectarian dispute has given us a

record (EC, 2. Inscriptions at Śravaṇa-Belgoḷa, No. 136) which narrates how king Bukkarāya of Vijayanagara brought about a reconciliation between the Jains and the Vaishṇavas of Śravaṇa-Belgoḷa, and embodies a compact under which the Jains were to enjoy equal freedom and protection with the Vaishṇavas in respect of their rites and processions.

The necessity for reforming the sacred law on a certain point has given us an inscription at Viriñchipuram (H.SII, 1. 82), embodying an agreement fixing the law of marriage among the Brāhmaṇs of the Paḍaivīḍu country, by which they bound themselves that marriages among their families should only be concluded by *kanyādāna*, that is to say, by the father giving his daughter gratuitously, and that any father accepting money, and any bridegroom paying money for his bride, should be subject to punishment by the king and excommunication from caste.

The desire of pilgrims to commemorate their visits to sacred sites has given us a number of records at Sāñchi (EI, 2. 87, 366) and at Bharaut (IA, 21. 225), which are of considerable value in the geographical line of inquiry.

And the presentation of caskets to hold relics of Buddha has disclosed to us, in the inscriptions found at the Bhattiprōlu Stūpa (see page 45 above), a peculiar variety of the Brāhmī alphabet, which has not been met with elsewhere, and which has an important bearing on the development of the art of writing in India.

C. Records of Religious Endowments

We come next to those inscriptions of which the object was to register donations and endowments made to gods, to priests on behalf of temples and charitable institutions, and to religious communities. **Records of religious endowments.**

The inscriptions of Aśōka, and of a king Daśaratha who according to the Purāṇas was his grandson, which are found in the caves on the Barābar and Nāgārjunī Hills (IA, 20. 361), were engraved to record the presentation of the caves to a community of Ājīvika ascetics.

The Nāsik inscription of Ushavadāta, son-in-law of the Kshaharāta king Nahapāna, dated in the year 42, in A.D. 120 (ASWI, 4. 102, No. 9; EI, 8. 82), was engraved to register the presentation of the cave, with endowments in money and with the gift of a coco-nut tree plantation, to a community of Buddhist monks.

The object of the Bhitarī pillar-inscription of Skandagupta (F.GI, 52), and of the Kūram grant of Paramēśvaravarman I.

(H.SII, 1. 144), was to register grants of villages to gods; in the first case to Vishṇu, and in the second case to Śiva.

The Indōr record of the time of Skandagupta, dated in A.D. 466 (F.GI, 68), was issued to record an endowment to provide oil for the lamp of a temple of the Sun.

Some of the charters of the early Kadamba kings of Banawāsi (IA, 6. 24 ff.; 7. 33 ff.) were issued to convey lands and villages to the god Jinēndra, and to members of various Jain sects for the maintenance of the worship of that god.

The object of the Kaluchuṁbaṟṟu grant of the Eastern Chalukya king Amma II. (EI, 7. 177) was to convey that village to a Jain teacher for the purposes of a charitable dining-hall of a Jain temple.

The principal record on the Ātakūr stone of A.D. 949–50 (EI, 6. 50) registers a grant of some land to a temple of Śiva, made in celebration of a fight between a hound named Kāḷi and a great wild boar, in which, while the hound slew the boar, the hound itself was killed.

The Cochin grant of Bhāskara-Ravivarman (EI, 3. 66), which establishes the existence of a colony of Jews in that part of India, was issued to record the bestowal of a village on the Jews, with the right to use certain religious paraphernalia.

But for the fact that the ultimate object of it was to register the names of the villages that were granted to Ēkāntada-Rāmayya for the purposes of a temple that he built, we should not have had the Ablūr inscription (EI, 5. 237; and see IA, 1901. 2), which discloses the real originator of the movement, in the twelfth century, that led to a local development of Śaivism, with renewed vigour, which resulted in the establishment of the sect of the Liṅgāyats or Vīra-Śaivas which occupies so prominent a position in the Beḷgaum, Bijāpūr, and Dhārwār Districts and in the northern parts of Mysore.

And so on with innumerable other instances, in which history has been recorded only as an incidental matter, in connexion with the primary topic of religious benefactions.

D. Records of Secular Donations

Records of secular donations.

Finally, we have the inscriptions which register secular grants, not in any way connected with religion, to private individuals. As a few instances here, we may cite the following.

The Halsī record of the Kadamba king Kākusthavarman (IA, 6. 23) registers the grant of a field, as a reward for saving his life, to a Sēnāpati or general named Śrutakīrti.

On the other hand, in recognition of an equally useful but

less laudable service, the supplementary inscription on the Ātakūr stone of A.D. 949–50 (see page 58 above) records that the Rāshṭrakūṭa king Kṛishṇa III. gave to the Western Gaṅga prince Būtuga II. the Banavase twelve-thousand province, and the districts known as the Beḷgoḷa three-hundred, the Purigeṟe three-hundred, the Kisukāḍ seventy, and the Bāgenāḍ seventy, as a reward for (so the record itself says) treacherously slaying the Chōḷa king Rājāditya in the act of embracing him in pretended friendship.

The Maḷavaḷḷi pillar-inscription of king Hāritīputta, of the Viṇhukaḍḍachuṭu line of the Sātakaṇi kings (EC, 7. SK, 263), was published to register the grant of a group of villages to a Brāhmaṇ. And the record of the Kadamba king Śiva-Skandavarman, on the same pillar (ibid., SK, 264), was published to renew that grant, and to confirm the enjoyment of it by a descendant of the original grantee.

The Mayidavōlu record of the Pallava king Śiva-Skandavarman, and the Koṇḍamudi record of Jayavarman (EI, 6. 84, 315), which have introduced to us a new archaic variety of the southern alphabet, were issued to register grants of villages to Brāhmaṇs.

The Paṭṭadakal pillar-inscription of A.D. 754 (EI, 3. 1), of special interest because it is a duplicate record in Nāgarī as well as in the local Kanarese characters, registers the grant of half a village to a Brāhmaṇ, with a subsidiary allotment of some land for religious purposes.

The Madhuban record of A.D. 630–31, of Harshavardhana of Ṭhāṇēsar and Kanauj (EI, 6. 155), was issued to cancel the tenure of a certain village under a forged charter, and to authoritatively assign the same village to two other Brāhmaṇs.

The Chammak record of the Vākāṭaka king Pravarasēna II. (F.GI, 235) was issued to grant that village to one thousand Brāhmaṇs, forty-nine of whom are named in it as the recipients appointed for the occasion.

The record on the Vakkalēri plates or Suḷḷiyūr grant of A.D. 757 (EI, 5. 200; and see page 27 above), which gives the full direct lineal succession of the Western Chalukyas of Bādāmi, from the first paramount king, Pulakēśin I, to the last of the line, was framed in order to register the grant of a village to a Brāhmaṇ.

The Doḍḍahuṇḍi inscription of about A.D. 840 (EI, 6. 41), which records the death of the Western Gaṅga prince Nītimārga-Raṇavikrama, was incised in order to register the grant of some land to one of his followers.

The Nīlgund inscription of A.D. 866 (EI, 6. 98) registers the fact that, under a royal decree of the Rāshṭrakūṭa king Amōghavarsha I, the tax on clarified butter or ghee was assigned to the Mahājanas or elders of the village; evidently in order to make the proceeds of the tax available for expenditure by them on communal purposes, instead of being credited to the royal revenues.

And the Paiṭhaṇ plates of A.D. 1272, an epigraphic curiosity in respect of their great weight (see page 33 above), were issued to convey certain villages to fifty-seven Brāhmaṇs.

Finally, in this class we have, amongst numerous other records, the majority of the *vīrgals* of Mysore, which, differing in this respect from the similar records elsewhere, mostly record grants of land in addition to commemorating the deaths of heroes. For instance, the inscription on the Bēgūr stone of the period A.D. 908–38 (EI, 6. 45) not only records the death of the commander of the Nāgattara troop in a battle that was fought between the forces of Ayyapadēva and those of Vīramahēndra, but also records the appointment of his successor, and registers the grant of various villages to him.

A second clause in the supplementary inscription on the Ātakūr stone of A.D. 949–50 (see pages 58, 59, above) gives another instance of a grant of villages in recognition of bravery in the battle-field, to a hero who fought and survived.

And we learn from this last record that grants of this kind were sometimes accompanied by the ceremony of washing the warrior's sword, just as religious grants were usually accompanied by the ceremony of laving the feet of the priest into whose hands the donation was actually given.

E. The Essential Nature of the Inscriptions

The essential nature of the inscriptions.

We have thus shown the general nature of the epigraphic records, by a rough classification of them according to the objects to which they were directed.

Now, the donative records are by far the most numerous of all. And, as the result of this, we arrive at the point that in the vast majority of the epigraphic records we have a mass of title-deeds of real property, and of certificates of the right to duties, taxes, fees, perquisites, and other privileges. The copperplate grants are the actual title-deeds and certificates themselves. The stone inscriptions are usually of the same nature, but they sometimes mention the concurrent bestowal of a copperplate charter. And in such cases they are, rather, a public intimation that the transaction had been made complete and valid by the private assignment of the necessary title-deeds and certificates.

The essential part of the records was, of course, the specification of the details of the donor, of the donee, and of the donation. And we have to bear in mind that, not only are the donative records by far the most abundant of all, but also, among them, by far the most numerous are those which we may call the records of royal donations; by which we mean grants that were made either by the kings themselves, or by the great feudatory nobles, or by provincial governors and other high officials who had the royal authority to alienate state lands and to assign allotments from the state revenues. The reason for this, no doubt, is that which was suggested by Dr. Burnell (B.ESIP, 94); namely, the tendency for gifts to take the place of the sacrifices which, according to the epic poems, and in fact according to some of the earlier records, the kings of India used to have performed in order to acquire religious merit, or to attain other objects. But, be the reason what it may, the fact remains, that the records of royal donations, whether for religious purposes or for other purposes, are the most numerous of all. And many of them register, not simply the gift of small holdings, but grants of entire villages, and large and permanent assignments from the public revenues.

It is to these facts that we are indebted for the great value of the records from the historical point of view. The donor of state lands, or of an assignment from the public revenues, must show his authority for his acts. A provincial governor or other high official must specify his own rank and territorial jurisdiction, and name the king under whom he holds office. A great feudatory noble will often give a similar reference to his paramount sovereign, in addition to making his own position clear. And it is neither inconsistent with the dignity of a king, nor unusual, for something to be stated about his pedigree in charters and patents issued by him or in his name. The precepts of the law-books, quoted by Dr. Burnell from the chapters relating to the making of grants, prescribe in fact that a king should state the names of his father, his grandfather, and his great-grandfather, as well as his own (B.ESIP, 97). That, no doubt, was a rule deduced from custom, rather than a rule on which custom was based. But we find that, from very early times, the records do give a certain amount of genealogical information. More and more information of that kind was added as time went on. And the recital of events was introduced, to magnify the glory and importance of the donors, and sometimes to commemorate the achievements of recipients.

Thus, not with the express object of preserving history, but in order to intensify the importance of everything connected with religion, and to secure grantees in the possession of properties conveyed to them, there was gradually accumulated almost the whole of the great mass of epigraphic records from which, chiefly, the ancient history of India is now being put together.

F. The great Number of the Inscriptions

The great number of the inscriptions.

It must be added that neither are the epigraphic records at all few in number, nor are they confined to any limited divisions of the country.

The inscriptions of India itself come from all parts: from Shāhbāzgarhī in the north, in the Yūsufzai subdivision of the Peshāwar District, to the ancient Pāṇḍya territory in the extreme south of the Peninsula; and from Assam in the east to Kāṭhiāwār in the west.

And there are also others, from beyond the confines of India, of which we must take account in our Indian researches. We have important records in the Indian mixed dialect, neither exactly Sanskṛit nor exactly Prākṛit, from Afghānistān, and others, in Sanskṛit, from Nēpāl; these are so intimately connected with India that they are always classed and treated amongst the Indian records. We have records as well as manuscripts from Central Asia, in some dialect of the mixed class, and not only in the Kharōshṭhī characters, which, though used in the north-west of India, were not, we have now learnt, confined to that territory, but also in the Indian Brāhmī characters[1]; the exploitation of this source of information has recently begun. From over the sea, we have Sanskṛit, Pāli, and Singhalese records from Ceylon, useful to us in the historical line as well as in the palaeographic and linguistic departments; the systematic examination and publication of these has now commenced in the *Epigraphia Zeylanica*. From Further India, we have Sanskṛit records from Cambodia in Indo-China, ranging onwards from A.D. 604[2]. Records in

[1] See, e.g., Dr. Stein's *Archaeological Exploration in Chinese Turkestan*, 37, 52, 55.

[2] These have been made known to us by M. Barth, in his *Inscriptions Sanscrites du Cambodge*, and by M. Bergaigne, in his *Inscriptions Sanscrites de Campa et du Cambodge*.

Sanskṛit come even from Java; six such, ranging from A.D. 732 to 1373, are already known (see IA, 4. 356; 24. 184 ff., Nos. 35, 42, 53, 57, 290). And we are beginning to obtain valuable records in Burma.

Further, the numbers of the records in India itself are very great. For India as a whole, a detailed list of the earlier inscriptions, anterior to about A.D. 400, is, it is understood, in course of preparation for the *Epigraphia Indica*: the already known inscriptions of that period number altogether, large and small, between 1,100 and 1,200; and, when once that list has been published, we shall be in a position to appreciate them far better than has ever yet been done. For Northern India, that is to say, chiefly for the territory lying to the north of the Narbadā and Mahānadī rivers, and for the period from about A.D. 400 onwards, Professor Kielhorn has given us a list (EI, 5. appendix), with dates, names, and some other leading details, of more than 700 inscriptions already known. And for Southern India, the same scholar has given us a similar list (EI, 7. appendix) of no fewer than 1,090 inscriptions, ranging onwards from about A.D. 500, the contents of which have already been sufficiently made known to be available for treatment in that way.

And, whereas new records are every year being freely obtained in Northern India, it is known that in Southern India there is a wealth of materials the extent of which can hardly yet be gauged. Sir Walter Elliott, who first systematically explored the southern records, with the result of the compilation of a manuscript collection of which copies exist in the Libraries of the Royal Asiatic Society and of the University of Edinburgh, collected transcriptions of 595 inscriptions from the Kanarese country, and a large number of others from the Telugu districts. Professor Hultzsch has given us, in his first two volumes of *South-Indian Inscriptions*, and in the first two parts of the third volume, critical texts and translations of some 300 records, chiefly from the Tamiḻ country. From the State of Mysore, Mr. Rice has brought to our notice some 9,000 records, in the volumes of his series entitled *Epigraphia Carnatica*. From the Beḷgaum and Dhārwār Districts, in the Bombay Presidency, ink-impressions of nearly 1,000 inscriptions were collected under the direction of the writer of this account; and the southernmost parts of Dhārwār, which abound with such materials, and some parts of the Beḷgaum and Bijāpūr Districts and of the Nizām's Dominions, still remain to be explored. And a great mass of materials from the eastern parts of Southern India lies ready to hand in the office of the Government Epigraphist.

G. The precise Dating of the Inscriptions

The precise dating of the inscriptions.

Further, we are not in any way left to grope our way blindly in the arrangement of this vast mass of materials. We have a definite guide in the fact that, from the first century B.C., the epigraphic records are for the most part specifically dated: some in the regnal years of well-known kings; others in the astronomical Kaliyuga reckoning, the initial point of which was placed in 3102 B.C.; and the large majority in the various historical eras, commencing with the so-called Vikrama era founded (see page 4 above, note 2) by Kanishka in 58 B.C. And with the specification of the year there are usually given details of the month, the day, etc., which sometimes enable us to state even to an hour the exact occasion of the framing of any particular record.

The initial points of all the eras are now well known. And we are now fully provided with tables which enable us to determine with accuracy, and without much trouble, the European equivalents, not only of the years, but also of all the other details of the Indian dates. Each worker, of course, will select for use, from amongst the various guides that are available, those tables with which he can work most quickly. But the following hints may be given to those who have still to take up this line of research.

For special expositions of most of the various eras, we have Professor Kielhorn's articles on the examination of questions connected with the Vikrama era of 58 B.C. (IA, 19. 20, 166, 354; 20. 124, 397); on dates of the Śaka era of A.D. 78 met with in inscriptions (IA, 23. 113; 24. 1, 181; 25. 266, 289; 26. 146); on the epoch of the Kalachuri or Chēdi era of A.D. 249 (IA, 17. 215); on the Harsha era of A.D. 605 or 606 (IA, 26. 29); on the Kollam era of A.D. 825 (IA, 25. 53, 174); on the epoch of the Nēwār era of A.D. 879 (IA, 17. 246); on the epoch of the Lakshmaṇasēna era of A.D. 1119 (IA, 19. 1); and on the Saptarshi era of Kashmīr, which has its initial point in 3076 B.C. (IA, 20. 149). And in the same line we have Mr. Shankar Balkrishna Dikshit's account of the twelve-years' cycle of the planet Jupiter (IA, 17. 1, 312; F.GI, appendix 3). For the Gupta-Valabhī era of A.D. 320, see F.GI, introd., 124.

For exactly accurate calculations, we have Professor Jacobi's tables for the computation of Hindū dates (EI, 1. 403; 2. 487; recast and simplified from an original article in IA, 17. 145), and Professor Kielhorn's tables for the sixty-years' cycle of Jupiter (IA, 18. 193, 380; 25. 233).

And for closely approximate calculations, sufficiently accurate in all ordinary circumstances, we have Dr. Schram's tables for the conversion of Hindū dates (IA, 18. 290), and the work of Mr. Sewell and Mr. Sh. B. Dikshit, entitled *The Indian Calendar*, with an appendix on eclipses of the sun in India by Dr. Schram, and with a supplement on eclipses of the moon in India by Mr. Sewell. This last-mentioned work, we may add, contains also tables for the computation of dates of the Muhammadan calendar; and, along with a general account of all the Hindū eras, it presents much useful information on the subject of the connected topic of Hindū astronomy.

We may finally mention, for light on various considerations that must be borne in mind in connexion with the details given in Hindū dates, Professor Kielhorn's article on festal days of the Hindū lunar calendar (IA, 26. 177).

V. General Observations and Indications of Lines of Future Research

General observations and indications of lines of future research.

We have thus explained and illustrated the value of the inscriptions of India. We have given an account of the substances on which they were recorded. And we have explained the essential nature of them, and have shown the precise reasons for which they are historically and chronologically so important.

For the most part the exploration of the inscriptions, and the collation of results from them, require nothing but intelligence and patience, coupled with a certain amount of experience. But there is one class of them which must be used with only the greatest caution, if at all.

Just as there are in India numismatic forgeries and (see IA, 30, 1901. 201, note 2) even literary forgeries, so also there are spurious, counterfeit, or forged records, as well as genuine ones. Some of these spurious records have imposed on us in the past. From accepting them, as well as from giving too ready a credence to the pseudo-historical legends which exist in abundance in so many parts of the country, and to the fantastic archives and Vaṁsāvalis, or successions of kings, of Orissa, and to similar documents obtained elsewhere (see page 8 above), and to imaginative chronicles such as the Koṅgudēśa-rājākkaḷ and the Rājāvalikathe (see page 6), much erroneous matter has been introduced into the history of India. And, in trying to prevent the introduction of any more such matter into it hereafter, as well as in eliminating the fables that have already been imported into it, we have to be specially on our guard against such materials as falsely purport to be ancient official records or vouchers issued by official authority.

While, however, we must thus indicate the existence of these spurious records, space does not permit of our entering into any details about them, and of accounting for the existence of them and showing how they may be detected. On these points reference can only be made to a full exposition of this matter given elsewhere (IA, 30, 1901. 201 ff.), with a list, which however is now not quite up to date, of the known records of this class. And in the same place there will be found a brief mention of certain other records, which also must only be used with discrimination. Some of these are, by their own admission, reproductions of original records; and we have to consider how far the originals may have been reproduced correctly, or may have been unintentionally perverted. Others of them, while not admitting that they are reproductions, plainly are such, or are reasonably suspected to be such. And there are also genuine records which have been tampered with (see ibid., 123, and note), in order to make them serve purposes other than those originally intended by them.

That matter we cannot enter into here. Nor is this the place for presenting any detailed exposition of the results that we have obtained from the genuine records.

The political history forms the subject of other contributions to this volume, and has also been treated in other ways elsewhere. For detailed accounts of different parts of India from this point of view, reference may be made to the present writer's *Dynasties of the Kanarese Districts of the Bombay Presidency*, in the *Gazetteer of the Bombay Presidency*, vol. i, part 2 (1896), pp. 277–584; to Dr. Bhandarkar's *Early History of the Dekkan*, in the same volume and part, pp. 133–275; and to Pandit Bhagwanlal Indraji's *Early History of Gujarāt*, in the same volume, part 1 (1896), pp. 1–206. We have, further, Mr. V. A. Smith's *Early History of India* (1904), wider in its title, but dealing chiefly with Northern India and requiring to be read with a knowledge of the views of other writers even for that part of the country. And for a general résumé of bases, with full references, arranged in such a way that the work will long remain indispensable to all students of Indian history, reference may be made to Miss Duff's *Chronology of India* (1899).

Thus, a great deal has already been done in the department of political history. Of course, many details still remain to be filled in from future exploration and research. But we have now a very fair knowledge of the ancient past of India from 58 B.C. to A.D. 320, and a comparatively copious knowledge of it from the latter time onwards. And we are indebted for this almost entirely to the inscriptions.

But, though so much has been achieved, a great deal still remains to be done even in the line of political history. And there are other departments of research, which must go hand in hand with the study of the inscriptions, in which hardly a beginning has been made, beyond a preliminary treatment, in detached writings, of details which will have to be hereafter brought together and handled on broader lines in connected and more easily accessible works.

A. The Inscriptions

In the first place, only a small part of the mine of epigraphic information has been as yet explored. For the earlier period, before A.D. 320, when the great Gupta dynasty of Northern India rose to power, we are looking forward to the results of excavations, still to be made, which should, and undoubtedly will, enable us to get at many an important record now hidden from sight. For the period onwards from that date, we have still to trace many additional copperplate records, not yet brought to notice, which unquestionably exist in private hands: and from the enormous number of stone records we have to select those which will best repay the trouble of editing them in full; dealing with the others by means of abstracts that shall bring forward every point in them that can be turned to practical account. **The inscriptions.**

As regards the earlier period, reaching back to the time of Buddha, we have one record, the inscription on the Piprahwa vase (see page 43 above), the oldest known Indian record, which may possibly date from within a century after the death of Buddha. We have a certain amount of epigraphic material of the time of Aśōka. We have some such material for the interval from his time to 58 B.C. We have a very appreciable amount of such material for the interval from that date to A.D. 320. And indications are not wanting that systematic exploration of judiciously selected sites, as well as chance discoveries, will greatly and quickly increase the number of instructive inscriptional records available for the whole period; we may point, for instance, to the results of the excavations recently made under the supervision of the Director-General of Archaeology at Sārnāth, Kasiā, and Basāṛh, which have well illustrated what important epigraphic remains may be found lying even close at hand within quite easy reach. Still, for the present, we are greatly dependent for our knowledge of that period upon coins, and upon tradition as preserved in literary works; both of these being sources of information which must be used with extreme care and discrimination. The explorations and the chance discoveries have still to be made, and the results of them have to be examined and weighed as they may come to light.

In the second place, we must before long make a start towards bringing the records together, in chronological order, in volumes according to the dynasties and periods to which they belong, on lines such as those adopted in the volume of *Gupta Inscriptions*, prepared by the writer of the present account as the third volume of the intended *Corpus Inscriptionum Indicarum*, which, however, has not as yet gone beyond that volume and vol. i, by General Sir Alexander Cunningham, which gave the first collective treatment of the records of the Aśōka period.

It is very difficult to exhaust any particular line of research from texts which are scattered about in the volumes of different journals, amongst extraneous matter of all sorts and without any attempt at, or possibility of, general arrangement according to dates, and many of which are printed in native characters which do not lend themselves to the use of capitals, thick type, and other devices for marking points that are to be specially attended to. To a great extent, of course, this scattered and unsystematic disposal of our results has been unavoidable. As an inevitable consequence, however, not even the department of political history has been dealt with as fully as might be the case even from such materials as we already have for reference. And, though much has been accomplished by the official journal, the *Epigraphia Indica*, towards minimizing the difficulties entailed by having to search the volumes of so many different publications, more still requires to be done.

We must set about bringing together, in the manner indicated above, such records as have already been published; inserting at the same time any others of each series that can concurrently be prepared for publication. We want, for instance, one volume devoted to the records of the Western Chalukyas of Bādāmi, with those of the early Kadambas of Banawāsi and the Pallavas of Conjeeveram, and with some others of the same period which are not numerous enough to make up a volume by themselves. We want another volume for the records of the Eastern Chalukyas; another for those of the Rāshṭrakūṭas; others for those of the Kalachuris and the Gāhaḍavālas; and so on; each with the miscellaneous records of the period brought in. When such compilations have been made, we shall have the basis of a systematic arrangement, by means of which the materials can be examined far more conveniently and exhaustively than at present. And it will then be an easy and simple matter to insert in such volumes, in the proper places, references to further records, which, of course, must continue to be published in the present detached manner until sufficient materials for supplementary volumes accumulate.

In thus rearranging the records already edited, we have to revise the published texts, and bring them up to date on a uniform system according to our latest knowledge and experience. Even among the most recently issued versions, there are but few that could be finally reprinted just as they stand. We require to have both the texts and the translations dealt with critically, according to a thoroughly consistent method of treatment. The same passages in different records have to be translated in identically the same words. And technical titles and expressions require to be recognized, and to be used as they stand without attempting to render them by English words which may, indeed, be literal translations, but the meanings of which do not suffice to convey the ideas intended by the originals. There are many points in the records which will not be recognized until we begin to deal with the records on the lines indicated above. There are also many allusions in the records which we are only now beginning to understand. And, as a very suitable instance of what an up-to-date revision can effect, we may point to the case of the Aihoḷe inscription of A.D. 634–35, of the time of the Western Chalukya king Pulakēśin II. It was first handled fully by the present writer some thirty years ago (IA, 5. 67; 8. 237). It seemed, then, that at any rate all the historical matter in it had been brought out fully and correctly. But it remained for Professor Kielhorn, in lately examining the record anew and re-editing it with the advantages of experience and wider knowledge (EI, 6. 1), to remove some mistakes then made, and to discover yet two more historical items in it, in the mention of the Kollēru lake and of the territory on the north of the Bhīmā, and, further, to detect and explain two recondite allusions, one to a grammatical rule of Pāṇini and the other to the traditional precepts for the behaviour of kings in exile, and to bring out various interesting points in which the writings of the poet Kālidāsa were used and imitated in this record and in some other early ones.

B. Tradition

Tradition. We have mentioned tradition, as preserved in literary works, as one of our sources of information; but with the reservation that, along with what we gather from coins, it must be applied with extreme care and discrimination.

We may fairly use tradition to help us to interpret obscure expressions in the inscriptions, and in a general way to explain the meaning and the bearing of those records. We may even use it to fill up gaps in the history deduced from the inscriptions, when nothing incongruous or improbable is suggested by it; especially when it receives, in respect of immediate surroundings, any specific corroboration from the inscriptions, as in the case of the interval from the death of Buddha to the anointment of Aśōka to the sovereignty, and in the case of the missions that were sent out by Moggaliputta-Tissa to establish the Buddhist faith in the border-lands (see pages 44, 54, above).

But, when we can gather plain facts from the epigraphic records and arrange them on the bases of those records, we are independent of tradition, and can then recognize it only with a view to gauging its value in the light of what we learn from the only definite source of information. And we must not, in any circumstances, twist the assertions of tradition. We must not start by conjecturally correcting its statements, just as fancy may dictate, in order to make them support that which we seek to prove. We must not, as a basis for our application of it, make it say what it does not say. We may correct it only when we have undeniable evidence that it is open to correction, and an unmistakable guide as to the direction in which it may be corrected.

The Buddhist tradition of the seventh century A.D., of India, Gandhāra, and Kashmīr, as reported by Hiuen-tsiang[1], placed the initial dates of Aśōka and Kanishka respectively 100 and 400 years after the death of Buddha. Applied to 264 B.C. as the initial date of Aśōka the Maurya[2], this gives us 364 B.C. as one amongst various more or less substantial traditional dates for the death of Buddha. With that, however, we are not here concerned. Our point is this. A combination of those state-

[1] For a full exposition of this matter, see JRAS, 1906. 979 ff.

[2] See ibid., 984 ff.

ments places the initial date of Kanishka 300 years after the initial date of Aśōka; with the effect, on the same application, of setting up A.D. 37 for the initial date of Kanishka. But that did not suit the views of certain writers who wished to make the initial date of Kanishka fall in or about A.D. 78: and, accordingly, they increased the traditional 400 years for Kanishka into 437 years, by applying the statements as if they gave for him an interval of 300 years from, not the initial date of Aśōka, but the end of his reign; so that, Aśōka the Maurya having reigned for thirty-seven years, from 264 to 227 B.C., they of course obtained A.D. 73 (a result quite close enough for their purposes) for the initial date of Kanishka. The key to the matter here is found in the Buddhist tradition of Ceylon, confirmed for India by a record of Aśōka himself. From those sources we know that the said tradition of India, Gandhāra, and Kashmīr, confused Aśōka-Dharmāśōka the Maurya, in respect of his date, with a predecessor, Aśōka-Kālāśōka the Śaiśunāga, who began to reign 90 years after the death of Buddha, and in whose eleventh year, 100 years after the death of Buddha, there was held the second Buddhist Council. From those sources we know, also, that the death of Buddha occurred 218 years before the initial date of Aśōka the Maurya; that is, in 482 B.C. And, applied to 482 B.C., the statement of 400 years for Kanishka places his initial date in 82 B.C. That is, we can now see, it is a statement in round numbers of 400 for 424 years; and the tradition is in perfect accordance with the fact that Kanishka founded the so-called Mālava or Vikrama era commencing in 58 B.C.[1].

Again, tradition, as recorded by Hiuen-tsiang, tells us as follows:—In the midst of the 1000 years after the death of Buddha[2], or within the 1000 years after the death of Buddha[3], there reigned at Śrāvastī a powerful and ostentatiously lavish king Vikramāditya, who ultimately lost his kingdom in consequence of behaving uncivilly to a Buddhist teacher named Manōratha, and was followed[4] by a successor who showed respect to men of eminence. Further, tradition, as recorded by the same writer, tells us[5] that in quite a different part of India, namely in Mālava, and about sixty years before the time (A.D. 641–42)

[1] See page 4 above, and note 2.

[2] Julien, *Mémoires*, I. 115; Beal, *Records*, I. 105.

[3] Julien, loc. cit., note 3; Watters, *On Yuan Chwang*, I. 211.

[4] Julien, loc. cit., 118; Beal, loc. cit., 118; Watters, loc. cit., 212.

[5] Julien, op. cit., 2. 156; *Vie*, 204; Beal, op. cit., 2. 261; *Life*, 148; Watters, op. cit., 2. 242.

when Hiuen-tsiang was writing, there was a king Śilāditya, who reigned for fifty years[1], and who, in addition to being a man of great wisdom and one who was attached to and beloved by his subjects, was full of respect for the three precious things of the Buddhist faith. These two accounts refer to very different parts of India. They were recorded on different occasions, and without any reciprocal connexion. And even the date of Vikramāditya of Śrāvastī still remains to be determined. Nevertheless, and because the result is supposed to fit in with a very liberal adjustment of some mythical statements, distinctly referred to the period about A.D. 78, made in the twelfth century by Kalhaṇa in the Rājataraṁgiṇī, 3. 125–331, about a king Harsha-Vikramāditya and his son Pratāpaśīla-Śilāditya of still a third kingdom, Ujjain, we have been told (JRAS, 1903. 565 ff.) that, while Hiuen-tsiang has reported the facts themselves correctly, he has confounded the two names, and what he relates about Vikramāditya of Śrāvastī really applies to Śilāditya of Mālava, but also, while we transfer Vikramāditya from Śrāvastī to Mālava, we are to leave Śilāditya in that same locality.

Results can be strung together from treatments of tradition such as the two cited above. But such results are not history.

We may use tradition. But we must weigh it, and must not distort it. We must see that we understand it aright. We must not take one line of it, say the Buddhist tradition of the Dīpavaṁsa of Ceylon, and modify it according to another line, say the Brāhmaṇical tradition of the Indian Purāṇas. And we must take care that whatever tradition we do use shall be ancient. We cannot base history upon fanciful collections of legendary matter, dignified by the name of tradition, presented to us in modern compilations such as the Koṅgu-dēśarājākkaḷ and the Rājāvalikathe (see page 6 above). And, in these days of dissemination of knowledge, we must be on our guard against admitting so-called traditions which are really the results of our own conjectures dressed up in other forms. In this direction, we have before us the notorious case of the bards of Kāṭhiāwār (see F.GI, introd., 49 f.). They have a story about the rise of Valabhī, which was at one time brought forward and accepted as 'an old-world tale' which had an historical basis, though it might not be altogether accurate. But it was subsequently made known that the story only sprang into existence some quarter of a century ago

[1] Julien, *Mémoires*, 2. 156; *Vie*, 205: Beal, *Records*, 2. 261; *Life*, 148.

and owed its origin entirely to modern speculations which had found their way to the bards through an educational treatise.

In short, it cannot be too steadily borne in mind that, while we may most suitably take tradition as a subsidiary source of history, we must weigh it carefully before we use it. It can in no way take the place of the epigraphic records. It is of no value against any plain and unmistakable assertions made by them.

C. Palaeography, Coins, and Art

Palaeography, coins, and art.

The palaeographic inquiry has been brought to a climax for the present by Professor Bühler's *Indische Palaeographie*. The German original of this invaluable work, with its plates, was published in 1896 as part xi. of the first volume of the *Grundriss der Indo-Arischen Philologie und Altertumskunde*, or Encyclopaedia of Indo-Aryan Research. And the English version of the letter-press of it has been issued as an appendix to the *Indian Antiquary*, vol. xxxiii, 1904.

But in this line, as also in the historical line, on which it is largely dependent, and, in fact, in every line of Indian research, we are steadily accumulating more facts and better materials, and making substantial progress every year. Already, some of the details exhibited in Professor Bühler's work might now be treated, or at least considered, from other points of view. Already the Mayidavōlu record of Śiva-Skandavarman and the Koṇḍamudi record of Jayavarman (see page 59 above) have given us a new archaic variety of the southern alphabet, which was not known when Professor Bühler was writing.

Even the palaeographic inquiry, therefore, has sooner or later to be taken a step farther than the high point to which it has been brought by the labours of Professor Bühler.

As one way of helping to this end, the occasions of publishing more advanced texts and translations of records already handled, must be utilized to substitute real facsimiles of at least the more representative originals, in the place of the manipulated and sometimes misleading lithographs that have occasionally been issued in times gone by. Then, attention was directed to publishing clear and easily legible lithographs, rather than to giving facsimiles which an unpractised eye might find it difficult to deal with because of their including all the imperfections of the originals due to damage and decay. Now, with greatly improved methods of preparing our materials for reproduction, we take a wiser course.

We require for critical work, in any line, purely mechanical reproductions, which shall be actual facsimiles of the originals as they stand, prepared without, at any stage, any touching up by hand of the materials, ink-impressions or uninked estampages, which are the bases of them, or of proofs from those materials. Any such touching up by hand of such materials, and any issuing of lithographs from eye-copies, gives us, not what really stands in an original but that which the operator thinks he sees there, which is often quite a different thing; and, for two pointed illustrations of this, reference may be made to some remarks by the present writer on another occasion (EI, 6. 80). Any such process deprives of all value the results that are laid before us. And it must be sedulously avoided, in the first treatment of any new materials, as much as in the revision of any old ones.

In connexion with this branch of the general inquiry, it must also be borne in mind that it is not easy to fix within a century or so, or even more, on simply palaeographic grounds, the time of an undated record which does not present the name of a well-known king, or some other specific guide. And of this there is on record a case in point that may be appositely cited. It has been said, and not unjustifiably (JRAS. 1903. 393), that the characters of the legend on a certain coin may be, perhaps, of the ninth or tenth century; leaving us to infer that the coin itself might be allotted to that time. But from the words of the legend, 'the glorious Rāya-murāri,' we know that the coin is one of the Kaḷachurya king Rāyamurāri-Sōvidēva-Sōmēśvara of Kalyāṇi (see F.DKD, 471), who reigned A.D. 1167–77.

There should further be borne in mind certain considerations which apply also to numismatic theories and views about art, as other bases for the construction of history.

In the case of royal proceedings and the records of them, we may expect that both the artistic standard of any statues or other sculptures chosen as objects of presentation, and of any shrines or other buildings ordered to be erected, and also the characters, drafting, etc., of the records of such acts, should ordinarily be the best procurable of their kind and time, and should be more or less uniformly progressive in one direction or another; in point of fact, it would seem, towards deterioration rather than improvement. But, even so, there must have been incidental times of throwing-back, and occasions when actually the best synchronous work in either line could not be obtained, even on royal demands. And the position must always have been very different in respect of private proceedings and the records of them; and we must remember that many of the records of the first century B.C. and the following two centuries, and particularly those which come from Northern India, are private non-official records of private non-official donations and foundations. There are, and there must always have been, everywhere, and in every line, of writing, sculpture, or any other branch of work, good and bad workmen, synchronously and in the same localities. The terms of workmen vary, and must always have varied, according to their skill and reputation. Not every ordinary individual can have afforded to employ, even if he knew, the most deft sculptor, to give him the highest art, or the best writer, to give him the most approved official or even non-official script of his time. And considerations of that kind, and of locality, and of the materials used, metal, stone, etc., as the case may be, quite as much as differences of time, may account for many of the difficulties experienced in some quarters, sometimes on palaeographic grounds, sometimes from other points of view, of construing, as belonging really to one and the same series, certain dates from Northern India which run harmoniously from the year 3 to the year 399 without any actual specification of the name of the era,—the so-called Vikrama or Mālava era, founded by Kanishka in 58 B.C.,—to which they belong.

So, too, as regards coins. The sinking of dies must always have been a somewhat close profession, transmitted hereditarily, and probably confined to but a few families, in but a few localities, the members of which would be summoned far and wide for the exercise of their skill. In this line, too, not always could the best work have been obtainable, even by a king. A new design, shape, or weight from Greece or Italy, or a new development of the Greek alphabet, may easily have reached Broach by sea, and may thence have travelled overland via Ujjain to Muttra, much more quickly than it could penetrate into India by way of Persia and the north-west frontier. Or, again, a new design, shape, or weight, originating in Persia, may have reached India long before it could reach Italy or Greece. And such conditions as these, coupled with a natural tendency to follow, if not exactly to copy, previous models, may account for many of the difficulties that attend the arrangement of numismatic facts.

In short, not only palaeographic views, but also numismatic theories and deductions based on art, must always be subordinate to, and must be regulated by, what we can learn in the way of clear facts from the inscriptional records.

D. Geography

Geography. As has been said, even the political history has not been yet worked out from the published records as fully as might be done. And there are other lines of inquiry, of general historical interest, particularly in the geographical, administrative, and fiscal departments, which have hardly been touched upon at all to any purpose.

The geography, indeed, an attractive branch of inquiry which has been popular in many quarters, has received a certain amount of attention. But the researches in this line have been made chiefly with the object of trying to identify places, countries, and tribes mentioned by foreign writers, namely, the Greek historians and geographers, the Chinese pilgrims, and the Arab travellers, and of constructing maps of ancient India from their writings. And in that connexion much has been put forward in vain, in consequence of an idea that we can and must still find an existing representative of every ancient name recorded by the foreign writers. But tribes die out and disappear; towns decay and are deserted; seaside emporia sometimes shift: and, in addition to the gradual transition from classical to vernacular forms, the names of cities are liable to change entirely in the course of time, even though the places themselves survive.

Some of the records of the Indian campaign of Alexander, in 327 to 324 B.C., were plainly based on accounts written by persons who actually went to India with him[1]. Yet but few of the places mentioned in them have been identified with any real approach to certainty.

The author of the Periplus of the Erythraean Sea[2], who wrote at some time about A.D. 85, evidently sailed in person round the coast of India. But we cannot expect to find now every place on the coast mentioned by him. And, as regards his

[1] See, in particular, *Ancient India, its Invasion by Alexander the Great* (1893), by J. W. McCrindle; and his *Ancient India as described in Classical Literature* (1901).

[2] For McCrindle's translation of this work see IA, 8, 1879. 107 ff. He has there shown grounds, which seem conclusive, for placing the work between A.D. 80 and 89, though by other authorities it has been placed somewhat earlier, in Pliny's time (A.D. 23 to 79), and, on the other hand, considerably later, after A.D. 161. The writer of the geographical part of the article on Ptolemy in the *Encyclopaedia Britannica*, vol. xx, has placed it 'about A.D. 80' (p. 94).

inland details, his statement that Paiṭhaṇ, which is really about 200 miles almost due south-east from Broach, lay south of the latter place, at a distance of a twenty days' journey, quite suffices to show that, for places away from the coast, he was at least sometimes dependent on information which was liable to be of a very vague kind; and it left us free to exercise considerable latitude of choice, fully justified when at length the identification came to be made (see page 82 below), in applying his immediately following assertion that Tagara, a famous inland emporium, situated at a distance of a ten days' journey from Paiṭhaṇ, was on the east of Paiṭhaṇ: the correct bearing is, in reality, as closely as possible south-east by south.

Ptolemy, who wrote approximately[1] at some time about A.D. 150, had not even the opportunities of personal observation which the author of the Periplus enjoyed, but only compiled from the reports of travellers and navigators, and from the works of previous writers, of whom some may have enjoyed such advantages, but others had simply put together information obtained similarly at second-hand. Consequently, it is only in a very general way, at any rate with merely our present means of applying the information given in his work[2], that we can use his statements towards reconstructing the early geography.

The writer of the geographical part of the article on Ptolemy in the *Encyclopaedia Britannica*, vol. xx, has told us that Ptolemy's geographical knowledge is strikingly imperfect even in regard to the Mediterranean and its surroundings, and that it is especially faulty in respect of the southern shores of Asia, in connexion with which he had obtained (as we can readily detect) only a vague acquaintance with extensive regions, based on information which was indeed to a certain extent authentic, but which had been much exaggerated and misunderstood. Ptolemy (we are told) recognized the importance of utilizing, to check and adjust results, any positions of places that had been determined by actual observations of latitude and longitude. But there was not any appreciable number of such places. And thus 'the positions laid down by him were really, with very few exceptions, the result of computations of distances from itineraries and the statements of travellers,

[1] It appears that the first-recorded observation of this celebrated mathematician, astronomer, and geographer was made in A.D. 127, and the last in A.D. 151 (*Encyclopaedia Britannica*, xx. 87); but that he was still alive in A.D. 161 (*Smith's Classical Dictionary*, 627).

[2] See *Ptolemy's Geography of India and Southern Asia*, with a commentary, by McCrindle, in IA, 13, 1884. 313-411.

estimates which were liable to much greater error in ancient times than at the present day.' Moreover, in addition to placing the equator at a considerable distance from its true geographical position, and accepting a prime meridian which made all his eastern longitudes about seven degrees less than they should have been, he made a still more serious mistake, which 'had the effect of vitiating all his subsequent conclusions,' in taking every degree of latitude, and of longitude measured at the equator, as equal to only 500 stadia or fifty geographical miles, instead of its true equivalent of 600 stadia or sixty miles. And, as the result of the last-mentioned error, 'if he had arrived at the conclusion from itineraries that two places were 5,000 stadia from one another, he would place them at a distance of ten degrees apart, and thus in fact separate them by an interval of 6,000 stadia.'

The curious and utterly erroneous conception of the shape of India formed by Ptolemy, is well shown by the map (IA, 13. between pp. 322, 323) which accompanies Mr. McCrindle's extracts from his work. And the general distortions that resulted from his data and method of work are admirably exhibited in an ingenious form in the *Encyclopaedia Britannica*, vol. xv, in plate 7, between pp. 516, 517, which shows Ptolemy's idea of the world superimposed upon an actual map of the corresponding portions of the world. His results, exposed in this way, place Paiṭhaṇ (on the Gōdāvarī) well out to sea in the Bay of Bengal. They make Ceylon an enormous island, stretching from below the equator to about the twelfth degree of north latitude, and covering the position of the northern half of Sumatra and of part of the Malay Peninsula, with a large area of the Bay of Bengal, including the Nicobar Islands. They make the Mahānadī river run over Siam and Cambodia. They make the Ganges run over the very heart of China, flowing towards the sea somewhere near Canton. They carry Palibothra, which is Patna (on the Ganges), to the east of a line from Tonquin to Pekin. And they make the Himālayan range, as represented by the Imaos and Emodos mountains, run north of Tibet, through the north of China, across the Yellow Sea and Korea, and into Japan.

It is obvious that, before we can do anything substantial with Ptolemy's work, in the direction of utilizing it for even the outlines of the early political geography of India, we need something more in the way of an exposition of it than even that which Mr. McCrindle has given us; and we require an adjustment of Ptolemy's results for India similar to that which Colonel Gerini has made (JRAS, 1897. 551) in respect of his results for the countries beyond the eastern confines of India. But it is also certain that, though we may gather from Ptolemy a fair quantity of general information about tribes and territorial divisions, no amount of adjustment will ever enable us to frame from his work a map of India that would be even approximately accurate in its details.

Passing on to a still more definite source of information, we find that much even now remains to be done in connexion with the writings of Hiuen-tsiang[1], who travelled through practically the whole of India between A.D. 629 and 645, and kept a very close record of his peregrinations.

The territorial divisions mentioned by Hiuen-tsiang are fairly easy to locate, more or less approximately, with the help of the epigraphic records. But his cities, or such of them as survive, are more difficult. Before his writings can be fully utilized, we want better readings and explanations than have even yet been offered of his place-names. We have to re-examine his movements from the point of view that 100 *li* denoted the time occupied in making a day's journey[2]; the said day's journey averaging very closely about twelve miles, but being actually determined in each case by such considerations as the nature of the country traversed, and the distances between villages, sarais, and other convenient halting-places, so that it might easily in ordinary circumstances be anything from ten to fourteen miles, and in exceptional cases might have even a wider range in either direction. In connexion with the point that the distances and directions given by him as from country to country are almost always the distances and directions from each capital to the next capital, we have to bear in mind, in the first place, that even a slight difference in bearings will lead to a wide divergence in position when the bearings are set out on a long line; and, in the second place, that, whereas it is impossible that every capital can have been due north, east, south, or west, or due north-east, north-west, south-east, or south-west, from the preceding capital, he

[1] See *Histoire de la Vie de Hiouen-Thsang* (1853), and *Mémoires sur les Contrées Occidentales par Hiouen-Thsang* (two vols., 1857–58), by M. Stanislas Julien, with an examination of the geographical results by M. Vivien de Saint-Martin; *Si-yu-ki, or Buddhist Records of the Western World* (two vols., 1884), and *Life of Hiuen Tsiang* (1888), by the Rev. Samuel Beal; and *On Yuan Chwang's Travels in India* (two vols., 1904–5), by Mr. Thomas Watters.

[2] On the Indian *yōjana* and the Chinese *li* as measures of itinerary distance, see JRAS, 1906. 1011 ff.

recognized no points of the compass beyond those eight, and very seldom, if ever, gave the bearings except as if they were due north, etc., or due north-east, etc. And, not only some cases of discrepancy between the *Records* and the *Life*, but also certain various readings which exist, are quite enough to show that both his bearings and his directions have not always been correctly transmitted to us.

We have by no means yet found (if we ever can find) every city and other place mentioned even by Hiuen-tsiang; and some of the most confidently asserted identifications of places spoken of by him are unquestionably wrong.

Take, for instance, the case of the capital of Kaliṅga, which he visited and mentioned without, apparently, recording its name. M. Vivien de Saint-Martin felt satisfied (*Mémoires*, 2. 395) that it is represented by Kaliṅgapaṭam on the coast, in the Gañjām District; an identification which was practically, if not absolutely, endorsed by Mr. Ferguson (JRAS, 1873. 252): while General Sir Alexander Cunningham arrived at the conclusion (AGI, 516) that it must be Rājamahēndri on the Gōdāvarī, the head-quarters of a subdivision of the Gōdāvarī District. But the information furnished by the epigraphic records makes it certain that it was neither of those two places. It was the city Kaliṅganagara, which dates back to at any rate the time of king Khāravēla in the second century B.C., and was from about A.D. 645 onwards the capital of the Gaṅga dynasty of Kaliṅga. And the place is now represented (see EI, 4. 187 ff.) by the villages Mukhaliṅgam and Nagarakaṭakam and the ruins between them, on the Vaṁśadhārā river, in the Parla-Kimeḍi Zamīndārī or estate, in the Gañjām District.

Take, again, the case of an ancient city in the Punjab, regarding the identity of which there has been almost as much speculation, with announcements of confident results in various directions, as in the case of the famous Tagara (see page 82 below.) Hiuen-tsiang visited the city in question, and has mentioned it as She-ka-lo, the old capital of the Cheh-ka, Ṭakka, country, and the seat of government of the great foreign invader Mihirakula about the commencement of the sixth century A.D. It is otherwise of interest as being the Śākala of the Mahābhārata, and the Sāgala of the Milindapañha, which latter work specifies it as the capital of king Milinda, whom it is customary to identify with the Graeco-Bactrian or Indo-Grecian king Menander, and to place in the second century B.C. And there would have been no difficulty in finding its modern representative long ago, if only the attempt had been made without starting by correcting the indication given by Hiuen-tsiang as to its position. Starting by making such a correction, Sir A. Cunningham felt satisfied (C.AGI, 179 ff.) that the site of this city is marked by the Sangla Hill in the Gujrānwāla District. And proceeding on the same lines, and taking us at least as far from the locality indicated by the Chinese pilgrim, Mr. Rodgers and Mr. Vincent Smith pronounced[1] that this city is apparently either Chiniōṭ or Shāhkōṭ in the Jhang District. In reality, however, as has now been proved by the present writer[2], Śākala, Sāgala, She-ka-lo, is Siālkōṭ, the chief town of the Siālkōṭ District.

That the writings of Hiuen-tsiang, as transmitted to us, are sometimes open to correction is, indeed, certain. For example, they tell us that, going above 200 *li* south-east from P'i-lo-shan-na, he arrived at a country (capital) named Kah-pi-t'a; and that then, going north-west for nearly 200 *li*, he reached a country (capital) named Ka-no-kü-she (Watters, I. 333, 340). Here there is undeniably some mistake: the text represents him as exactly retracing his steps, and yet arriving at a totally different place. But, even with a various reading which gives the bearing from Kah-pi-t'a to Ka-no-kü-she as south-east instead of north-west, we must not jump too readily to the conclusion that that is the detail in which the mistake lies. Before we can approach that point, we must determine, more definitely than has yet been done, the exact position of Kah-pi-t'a, and make sure that the mistake does not lie in the specification of the direction of that place from P'i-lo-shan-na.

With the writings of Hiuen-tsiang we shall be able to do much more than has hitherto been done, if we refrain from the prima-facie assumption that his statements are open to correction freely, and if, when we find cases like the above in which there is certainly some mistake, we weigh all the surroundings more fully, instead of forming a preconceived notion and then making the correction in accordance with it.

And there are other writings which are likely to be of considerable use, if we are given the means of looking behind certain restorations which have been made in the treatment of them. For instance, a fair amount of geographical information is to be found in Alberūnī's work on India, written in A.D. 1031–32. But, in order that the work may be fully utilized, not only in this direction but in others also, by those who do

[1] *Early History of India*, 65, note, and 274.

[2] *Fourteenth Oriental Congress*, 1905, Algiers; Indian Section, 164 ff.

not read Arabic, we need something more than what has been given to us even by Professor Sachau's admirable translation, and by the index of words of Indian origin which accompanies his edition of the text. It is not enough for us to have the Indian place-names and other words restored into Sanskṛit forms, actual or conjectural; we require an index which shall give us exact transliterations of the names, etc., as presented by Albērūnī in Arabic characters. He has cited, to a large extent, Prākṛit rather than Sanskṛit forms; and it is the Prākṛit forms which are so useful to us in tracing transitions from the Sanskṛit to the modern forms.

For the ancient geography, in short, as for everything else connected with the past of India, we are really dependent primarily and almost entirely on the epigraphic records. It is from that source that it must be mostly worked out. And we can only fill in additional details from extraneous sources, such as those discussed above, when we have arrived at some more definite idea of at least the general features from the indigenous materials.

The first desideratum now, in this line, is to index the published epigraphic records for all geographical details, and to prepare from them, and from such other native sources as can be conveniently worked in at the same time, an atlas of ancient India, a series of maps illustrating successive periods, which shall take the place of the long-since obsolete maps that are now available. Only in such a collection of maps shall we find the first reliable means of proceeding to apply properly any information that may be derivable from foreign sources. Many a result, advanced in the earlier inquiries indicated above, will be corrected in the course of compiling such a collection of maps; partly on the basis of better information already available, partly as the natural consequence of the care and thought that must attend the preparation of the compilation, if it is properly taken in hand. And many an interesting identification will be made at the same time, by the same means. It was only recently that the writer of the present account was able to show (JRAS, 1901. 537 ff.) that the ancient and famous Tagara exists to this day, known by the natural modern form of its former name, as Tēr, in the Nizam's Dominions (the misspelt Thair, Ther, Tair, of maps, etc.), though for more than a century of search and speculation its identity had escaped recognition. It is only still more lately that he has been able (see EI. 7. 223 ff.) to mark Lātūr in the same territory as the ancient Lattalūr, Lattanūr, the original home of the Rāshṭrakūṭa kings of Mālkhēḍ, and to prove (see page 80 f. above) that Siālkōṭ in the Punjab is the ancient city Śākala, Sāgala, mentioned as She-ka-lo by Hiuen-tsiang.

There are, however, also other urgent desiderata in connexion with our geographical inquiries [1]. A great obstacle to making identifications—in some cases a factor which directly leads to erroneous results—is the difficulty of ascertaining the real forms of the modern place-names. Official spellings are of little, if any, value; there is no system, in ordinary official use, which gives us the critical details that we require. We need a series of compilations for the various Presidencies and other territorial divisions of India, framed on the lines followed in the official manual entitled *Bombay Places and Common Official Words* (1878), but prepared in a thoroughly critical manner and as the result of skilled inquiry, which shall give us, in the native characters as well as in transliteration, the actually correct forms of the modern names of all the principal towns, villages, rivers, and mountains. And, to supplement those compilations, we need others similar to, and arranged like, the *Postal Directory of the Bombay Circle* (1879), which shall show, in alphabetical order and in transliteration only, the name of every town and village in each postal circle, with its district, subdivision, and post-town.

E. Other Fields of Work

There is, thus, plenty of both original research and revisional work still to be done in connexion with, and by the help of, the epigraphic records. And the leading desideratum is, certainly, to get those records explored more fully and published in larger numbers. **Other fields of work.**

But systematic co-operation in other lines of study would help very greatly, even towards a more accurate understanding of the records. And there are various ways in which much valuable assistance towards the ends that we have in view might be given by scholars who are not inclined to undertake the editing of the records, or even the detailed study of them.

In connexion with the general literature, there is still a great deal to be done in discovering, and bringing to notice by texts and translations, the historical introductions and colophons, the value of which has been indicated above (see page 19 ff.). Such materials are found freely in Southern India at any rate,

[1] For some fuller remarks on this topic, with an indication of the proper process to be followed in determining the true forms of modern place-names, see the observations by the present writer in JRAS, 1901. 549 ff.

and particularly in the Kanarese country. And results already published promise well for the future in this field of work.

We want a compilation of all the historical and geographical hints, and any other practical matter, that can be derived from the epics, the plays, the classical poems, and the collections of imaginative stories. And we want succinct abstracts of all the similar matter contained in the historical romances.

Life is too short for either the epigraphist or the historian to examine all these sources of information in the original texts, or even, in every case, to go thoroughly through translations of them. An editor of a text, on the other hand, could do all that is wanted in a day or two of extra work, the results of which would be embodied in an introduction and an index. And a student of any particular book might, on finishing his perusal of it, easily put together an instructive and valuable note which would be welcomed as an article in, for instance, the *Indian Antiquary*, in the pages of which it would at once attract the attention of those who could use it for general purposes.

The Paṭṭāvalis, the lists of the succession of the Jain pontiffs (see page 7 f. above), require to be examined more fully, especially with a view towards determining how far back we can carry the verses on which the earlier portions of them were based, and to what extent those portions of them are imperfect or erroneous and open to adjustment.

The geographical lists of some of the Purāṇas still remain to be exhibited, on lines similar to those adopted by the present writer in respect of the topographical list of the Bṛihat-Saṁhitā (IA, 22. 169). As yet we have, beyond that, only the list of the Bhāgavata-Purāṇa (IA, 28. 1). And, though it may be difficult to find many such lists the value of which is enhanced and made specific by our knowing the exact periods during which they were composed, as is the case with the list of the Bṛihat-Saṁhitā, still they will all come in usefully in some way or another. And there is, no doubt, many a Māhātmya or Sthalapurāṇa which will be useful for local geography and the identification of places, in the manner in which the Mahākūṭa-Māhātmya helped the writer of this account to establish the identity of the Vātāpi of the records, the capital of the great Chalukya dynasty of Western India, with the modern Bādāmi (IA, 5. 68; 8. 238).

We want a thorough exploration of all these subsidiary sources of information. And we want eventually a series of indexes to them similar to that prepared by Dr. Sörensen, and now in course of publication, of the names in the Mahābhārata; but bringing together also all the information that can be gathered from them in respect of social customs, trade and commerce, administration, arts and industries, and all the other lines of inquiry which present themselves to different workers in various fields of research.

The Mahābhārata—a vast repository, not simply of theories about cosmogony and time and space, of lectures on the duties of the castes, and of philosophical disquisitions, but also of ancient tales and legends to which there are constant references in the inscriptions, of geographical details, and of many other practical matters—will, in some respects, be exhausted by Dr. Sörensen's work.

But the Rāmāyaṇa remains. We want an index for that. We want another for the Vēdas. We want others for the Kāvyas, the dramas, the prose romances whether historical or fictitious, the Rājataraṁgiṇī, and any other works of that class. In the Buddhist division, we want indexes for the Dīpavaṁsa and the Mahāvaṁsa, for the writings of Buddhaghōsha, for the Jātaka, the Lalitavistara, and the Divyāvadāna, and for many another work which cannot be indicated here. So, also, we want indexes of the Jain and other Prākṛit works. And in the vernacular division we want indexes of, for instance, the Pampa-Bhārata, the Pampa-Rāmāyaṇa, and any other Kanarese works which, issued in print, are available for treatment.

But the field is a vast one, and can be properly worked only on the principle of co-operation of labour, by breaking it up into manageable areas.

F. Concluding Remarks

There is, in short, a vast amount of work still to be done, and by no means only in connexion with the inscriptions, but in all the various lines of research connected with the past of India. Concluding remarks.

We hope indeed, in particular, that the present exposition of the inscriptional bases of Indian research, and the accompanying sketch of the position at which we have arrived, may do something towards attracting more attention to the principal materials, the epigraphic records, and towards inducing more scholars to join us in exploiting them.

The means for carrying on this, the most essential, branch of the inquiry are ample. There is a special official journal, maintained expressly for the critical editing of the texts of the inscriptions, with translations of them, and with such explanatory comments as can be appropriately given with the texts, instead of being worked up into special articles of greater length in the *Indian Antiquary* and in the journals of the various learned societies. That journal is the *Epigraphia Indica*, started in 1888 or 1889, and now in its eighth volume. It is in the charge of an editor whose duty and pleasure it is to welcome all contributions to it, to advise and encourage novices, and generally to co-operate in the satisfactory publication of all communications sent in to him for it. And by the size of its pages, and the freedom with which facsimiles are issued to accompany articles in it, it is better suited than any other journal to the preliminary exploration of the inscriptions, as a necessary precursor of an ultimate grouping of them in the volumes of the *Corpus Inscriptionum Indicarum.*

The pages of that journal have been filled to good purpose by those who have already been engaged in this line of work. But we want more workers to join us. And we look for recruits specially to the class of scholars who have a certain knowledge of Sanskṛit to start with; because, though most of the records are not in Sanskṛit, that tongue is more or less the key to the languages in which they were written, and a general knowledge of Sanskṛit literature and mythology is essential to a proper understanding of many of the allusions in the records.

At the same time, anyone who has made himself conversant with one of the vernaculars in its archaic form and ancient literature, has necessarily acquired, by that process, a considerable acquaintance with the Sanskṛit vocabulary, and can easily master, by general reading, what else is wanted. A preliminary knowledge of Sanskṛit itself, therefore, is by no means absolutely indispensable. As regards other leading languages, in Kanarese at any rate we have, in the Rev. F. Kittel's Kannaḍa-English Dictionary (1894) and Grammar of the Kannaḍa Language (1903), two most scholarly and admirable compilations, which have now placed it in the power of all western students to understand fully, and do justice to, the beauties of that highly polished and powerful tongue; and in the three volumes of Dr. Hultzsch's *South-Indian Inscriptions* we have a number of carefully edited versions, a study of which would go far towards removing any difficulties in the way of grappling with the epigraphic peculiarities of Tamiḻ.

It is no specially difficult matter now to approach the epigraphic records. And a very brief study of some of the versions that have been most recently edited, and of the results brought forward from them, would quickly teach the lines on which it is desirable to deal with the records so as to produce the uniformity of treatment that is requisite, and would inevitably awake an interest that would induce a steady desire to join in the work that we have in hand. But we hope, also, that others may be induced to co-operate, by examining more methodically and critically the subsidiary sources of information, and by bringing forward their results in such a way as to make them available for being easily worked in with the more special results derivable from the epigraphic records.

The principal materials are the epigraphic records, the inscriptions. And a very brief study of some of them will suffice to show the specific importance of them, and to excite a desire to join in exploring them. But the subsidiary materials, also, are numerous and interesting. And anyone who will take any of them in hand systematically, with just enough knowledge of the results derived from the inscriptions to show the objects that require to be kept in view and the general lines of work that should be followed, can render assistance the value of which will be made clear enough when his results are put forward in an accessible form, even if it may not be fully realizable by him while he is actually at work.

J. F. FLEET.

List of Abbreviations

AR . . = *Asiatic Researches*; vol. i (1788) to vol. xx (1836-39).

ASI . . = *Reports of the Archaeological Survey of India*; CUNNINGHAM'S Series, vol. i (1871) to vol. xxiii (1887); general index by V. SMITH (1887).

ASSI . = *Reports of the Archaeological Survey of Southern India*; vol. i (1887), *The Buddhist Stupas of Amaravati and Jaggayyapeta*, by BURGESS; vol. vi (1894), *South-Indian Buddhist Antiquities*, by REA.

ASWI. = *Reports of the Archaeological Survey of Western India*; BURGESS'S Series, vol. i (1874) to vol. v (1883).

B.ESIP = BURNELL, *Elements of South-Indian Palaeography*; 2nd edition (1878).

C.AGI = CUNNINGHAM, *Ancient Geography of India, the Buddhist Period* (1871).

C.BT . = CUNNINGHAM, *The Bhilsa Topes* (1854).

C.IA . = CUNNINGHAM, *Inscriptions of Asoka*; *Corpus Inscriptionum Indicarum*, vol. i (1877).

C.MG. = CUNNINGHAM, *Mahabodhi-Gaya*, i.e. *Mahabodhi, or the Great Buddhist Temple under the Bodhi Tree at Buddha-Gaya* (1892).

C.SB . = CUNNINGHAM, *The Stupa of Bharhut* (1879).

EC . . = *Epigraphia Carnatica*, RICE's Series; vol. i (1886) to vol. viii (1904), vols. ix, x (1905), vol. xi (1903), vol. xii (1904).

EI . . = *Epigraphia Indica*; vols. i (1892) and ii (1894), edited by BURGESS; vol. iii (1894–95) and following ones, biennially, up to date, edited by HULTZSCH.

F.DKD = FLEET, *The Dynasties of the Kanarese Districts of the Bombay Presidency* (1896), in *The Gazetteer of the Bombay Presidency*, vol. i, pt. 2, pp. 277–584.

F.GI. = FLEET, *Gupta Inscriptions*, i.e. Inscriptions of the Early Gupta Kings and their Successors; *Corpus Inscriptionum Indicarum*, vol. iii (1888).

H.SII. = HULTZSCH, *South-Indian Inscriptions*; vol. i (1890), vol. ii (1891–95), vol. iii, pt. 1 (1899), pt. 2 (1903).

IA . . = *Indian Antiquary*; vol. i (1872) to vol. xiii (1884), edited by BURGESS; vol. xiv (1885) to vol. xx (1891), by FLEET and TEMPLE; vol. xxi (1892) and following ones, up to date, by TEMPLE.

JA . . = *Journal Asiatique*; vol. i (1822), and following ones up to date.

JAOS . = *Journal of the American Oriental Society*; vol. i (1849), and following ones up to date.

JASB . = *Journal of the Asiatic Society of Bengal*; vol. i (1832), and following ones up to date.

JBBRAS = *Journal of the Bombay Branch of the Royal Asiatic Society*; vol. i (1841–44; reprinted 1870), and following ones up to date.

JRAS . = *Journal of the Royal Asiatic Society*; first series, vol. i (1834) to vol. xx (1863); new series, vol. i (1865) to vol. xxi (1889); subsequent volumes, no series or numbers, annually, from 1890 up to date.

PSOCI = *Pali, Sanskrit, and Old-Canarese Inscriptions from the Bombay Presidency and parts of the Madras Presidency and Maisur*; a collection of 286 photographic and lithographic reproductions of inscriptions, compiled by FLEET and BURGESS, with an explanatory analysis by FLEET, and largely based upon a collection of photographs of inscriptions in Mysore made by DIXON and published in 1865, and upon similar photographs in HOPE's *Inscriptions in Dharwar and Mysore* (1866), and *Architecture in Dharwar and Mysore* (1866).

VOJ . = *Vienna Oriental Journal*, sometimes cited as WZKM, i.e. Wiener Zeitschrift für die Kunde des Morgenlandes; vol. i (1887), and following ones up to date.

ZDMG = *Journal of the German Oriental Society*, Zeitschrift der Deutschen Morgenländischen Gesellschaft; vol. i (1847), and following ones up to date.